THE GERMAN
IDEOLOGY

THE GERMAN IDEOLOGY

A NEW ABRIDGEMENT

Karl Marx
and
Friedrich Engels

Edited and with an
introduction by
Tom Whyman

Published by Repeater Books

An imprint of Watkins Media Ltd

Unit 11 Shepperton House

89-93 Shepperton Road

London

N1 3DF

United Kingdom

www.repeaterbooks.com

A Repeater Books paperback original 2022

1

Distributed in the United States by Random House, Inc., New York.

Introduction copyright © Tom Whyman 2022

Copyright © Repeater Books 2022

ISBN: 9781913462956

Ebook ISBN: 9781913462963

Printed and bound in the United Kingdom by TJ International Ltd

CONTENTS

1 Introduction by Tom Whyman

25 The German Ideology

27 Preface

29 1. "The Chapter on Feuerbach" or: "Some Notes Which Aren't Actually on Feuerbach, But Which Were at One Stage Fudged into a Chapter Called 'Feuerbach'", or: "Materialism as Philosophical Therapy: Towards the Constant Overthrow of All Existing States of Affairs".

88 2. "III. Sankt Max", or: "The Chapter on Stirner (Heavily Abridged)", or: "On Egoism and Class Consciousness".

196 3. Boiling Down Everything as Far as It Will Go: Abridgement of My Abridgement

231 4. Abridgement of the Abridgement of the Abridgement (from "Theses on Feuerbach")

232 Acknowledgements

INTRODUCTION
BY TOM WHYMAN

(1)

There are two stories that you might have heard about what *The German Ideology* is.

The first is that *The German Ideology* is the name of a text written by Karl Marx and Friedrich Engels in around 1846, when they were living in Brussels: the pair's final reckoning with the "philosophical tradition", before they overcame philosophy decisively — first with *The Communist Manifesto* (1848), then with Marx's crowning opus *Capital, Vol. 1* (1867). But, as with so many of Marx and Engels's writings, *The German Ideology* was never published in the lifetime of either. After an agreement they had to publish the manuscript collapsed, the authors simply shrugged their shoulders, decided the thing was mostly valuable as a work of "self-clarification" anyway, and — as Marx would later relate in his Preface to *A Critique of Political Economy* — abandoned it perfectly "willingly" to "the gnawing criticism of the mice".

Luckily, however, the manuscript wasn't *literally* eaten by mice (although some pages of the real, physical thing do apparently feature a few marks which look suspiciously like mice-bites) — as, in the wake of the Soviet revolution, it was rediscovered by researchers at the Marx-Engels Institute in Moscow, led by David Riazanov, who managed to prepare an edition for publication — though Riazanov himself fell victim to Stalin's purges in 1931. Upon its emergence, it became clear that *The German Ideology* had been a genuinely ground-breaking work, in which Marx and Engels had outlined their "materialist" theory of history — not only for the first time, but also more lucidly than they would ever manage again. This was no mere work of private self-clarification: it was a genuinely invaluable edition to the Marxist — indeed, the *philosophical* — canon. This text typically remains the focus of undergraduate philosophy courses on Marx to this day (much more so than *Capital*, for instance — which can, understandably, feel a bit too much like economics).

The second story goes a bit differently. According to this story, Marx and Engels did indeed set out to write a grand work called *The German Ideology*, which would have represented their final confrontation not only with the idealist philosophy of their day, but also the philosophical pretensions of various other socialist authors. But it was never finished, was not even exclusively written by Marx and Engels — bits of the "work" were contributed by the pair's Brussels socialist friends Joseph Weydemeyer and Moses Hess — and was later carved up by the authors for all sorts of different purposes. Parts of the manuscript — such as the chapter on one of the leaders of the Young Hegelians, Bruno Bauer — were published in obscure socialist journals while Marx and Engels were still alive, while the alleged chapter on the post-Hegelian materialist philosopher Ludwig Feuerbach, which had been held up as the most important part of the work, was in fact no such thing at all — it had rather been "constructed", by Riazanov and his colleagues, out of various fragmentary notes. A compelling case for this second story is presented by Terrell Carver and Daniel Blank in two books from 2014 — *A Political History of Marx and Engels's German Ideology Manuscripts* and *Marx and Engels's German Ideology Manuscripts: Presentation and Analysis of the Feuerbach Chapter*. It has also informed the production of a new German-language edition of the text, which was published as part of the MEGA2 (that is, "*Marx-Engels Gesamtausgabe 2*") project in 2017.

Of course, you might quite understandably be thinking: in the light of that second story, why have I even bothered to tell you the first one at all? Here we have two tales. One of them — the second — is, as far as anyone seems to be able to tell, the "truth", while the first is really just a nice little fantasy, which we now know, almost certainly, to be wrong. It's like a fairy tale. *The German Ideology*, as we tend to *think* we know it at any rate, is somehow unreal. Carver and Blank compare it to *The Will to Power*, Nietzsche's alleged *magnum opus*, which was in fact collated from some leftover notes by his proto-Nazi sister.

But this idea — that *The German Ideology*, and in particular the chapter on Feuerbach, does not "really" exist, and thus has an at best dubious scholarly validity — is one that I find troubling in the extreme. For *The German Ideology* is a text of rare power: the rare sort of philosophical tract that, when you read it, can make you feel ecstatic with the rush of thinking, the bright brilliant naming and unlocking of the reality which is otherwise stuck inchoate all around you. In *The German Ideology*, Marx and Engels diagnose the philosophy of Hegel and his successors as being ultimately in some sense the product of their mistaken identification of ruling-class ideology with objective reality — a mistake which will inevitably turn even the most ostensibly "radical" thought into reactionary tilting at windmills. The remedy to this is a thought which proceeds not *moralistically* — treating human beings as we, nowadays, think they *should* be — but materially: taking them as they actually, practically *are*. This way of seeing brings communism into view, as the name of the "real movement" that "abolishes the present state of things": the movement, that is, through which the urban working classes — the proletariat — will soon find themselves powerful enough not only to overcome the rule of their bourgeois masters, but also — both *in and through* this overcoming — to abolish the premises on which their own identity, *as* proletarians, rests. The end result — if this even counts, formally, as any sort of "end" at all — will be the liberation of everyone, into a really and fully *human* way of being.

Invalidating *The German Ideology* as having merely been "constructed by Riazanov", then, might possibly get us closer to "the truth" as considered from the perspective of Marx-Engels scholarship. But it risks taking us further from "the truth" *as such* — the truth of who we are, and the world that we live in; the truth, in short, as it might matter to people who are not Marx scholars (indeed — one would hope that the truth in this sense matters a great deal to Marx scholars as well!). In light of this, a better comparison than to the *Will to Power* might be Paul's *Epistle to the Hebrews*. Biblical scholarship has shown — beyond much doubt, as far as I understand things — that Paul was not in fact the author of *Hebrews*: in both style and content, it is simply too different to the letters we know for sure are his. But that doesn't mean that *Hebrews* shouldn't be included, among his epistles, in the Bible: in fact, the text is generally regarded as a theological masterpiece — in part precisely *because* Paul, whose Greek was invariably more functional than beautiful, didn't write it. Lots of important texts are "constructed" by a bunch of different authors, some seen, some unseen — authenticity is only one criterion of value.

(2)

This abridgement is intended, at least in part, as a way of responding to these textual concerns. It is possible, after all, to get lost in scholarly difficulties, to the point that one is no longer able to catch sight of the important ideas which motivate them. *The German Ideology*, if it is anything, is a text which contains an unusually concentrated number of incredibly important ideas. So I want to help us find a way out of the woods.

In short: I have decided to take these textual problems as an excuse to be creative. If the text of *The German Ideology*, as we have it, was always already an "editorial construction", the salvaging of a planned work based on bits of what Marx and Engels wrote towards it, with a central chapter assembled Frankenstein-like from notebooks, then that gives any new editors licence — I believe — to push concerns about how "authentic" they may or may not be being to the "true" text to the back; and instead devise a text that does the fullest justice, as they as the individual editor sees things, to the philosophical ideas contained therein. We should *not* proceed, that is, as if there is something holy about Marx and Engels' writings — as if they were somehow divinely inspired. This is a fraught task, and it is certainly one that might be undertaken either well or badly — one assumes, in doing it, the burden of getting things very wrong indeed. But this is how, today, I believe one might do the greatest justice to Marx and Engels's ideas.

The present edition reflects this conviction in the following ways. Firstly, I have cut down the thing traditionally known as the "Feuerbach" chapter to what I believe are its barest essentials, providing the reader with the tightest exposition of Marx and Engels's materialist philosophy of history possible.

Secondly, I have given this same treatment to an often neglected part of the text. Traditionally, almost all of the critical attention given to *The German Ideology* has focused on the material collated by Riazanov under the name "1. Feuerbach". Indeed: almost all existing abridgements of *The German Ideology* — C.J. Arthur's 1970 abridgement;

the versions of the text found in various editions of Marx's "Collected Writings", or "Early Writings" — give either *mostly* or *only* extracts from the "Feuerbach" section. And yet: the "Feuerbach" material — most of which is not, to be clear, in any sense "about" Feuerbach — in fact comprises only a pretty small part of Marx and Engels' *German Ideology* writings overall. In the version included in the *Marx-Engels Collected Works*, as published in English by Lawrence & Wishart, after the chapter on Feuerbach, there is a short chapter on Bruno Bauer. Along with a brief "Preface", these chapters, taken together, comprise just 93 pages. They are then followed by the third chapter, "Sankt Max", on the nihilist/egoist philosopher Max Stirner. This chapter is a vast 333 pages long. Together, these three chapters comprise "Volume 1" of *The German Ideology* as we have it; what we have of "Volume 2", on the so-called "True Socialists", is just over 100 pages long. So, by a comfortable distance, Marx and Engels' *German Ideology* writings are in fact *mostly* about Max Stirner.

This raises the question: just what's in the Stirner section, then? A question which really must be followed by a second one: why on Earth did Marx and Engels write so much about Stirner? Well, as it turns out, if you actually sit down and read the thing: there is plenty there of real value, particularly to anyone interested in questions pertaining to the relationship between Socialism and Egoism (or individualism), and the relationship between revolutionary ideology and morality. The problem, however, is that this material — valuable though it is — is not necessarily presented in any sort of readily legible or coherent form. The Stirner section essentially consists of (far too many) pages of notes towards a critique of a thinker who is, yes, notable for his influence on Marxist and anarchist thought, but who independent interest in has rarely extended much further than a small cabal of enthusiasts. While some stretches of the text are *relatively* polished, the bulk of these notes are rough and sloppy, and no one seems to have done any of the sort of editorial work on them that strikes me as being vital, to make them presentable to all but the most dedicated and specialist reader. I have therefore taken it upon myself to compress the Stirner section into as few pages as I might coherently extract from it, while also rather liberally cleaning up what I have extracted, to produce a version of the chapter that other people might (a) actually enjoy to read, and (b) find easy to understand.

My approach here is informed by my intended audience. As an abridgement, of course, this text is not really intended to be consumed by specialist scholars of Marx — even if, by setting out the text in the way that I have chosen to, I am effectively asserting a reading of Marx. This is first and foremost a *popular* edition of *The German Ideology*, intended for interested students and lay people, as well as academics distant enough from Marx scholarship to feel able to simply *dabble* in his writings: people who can feel free not to be completionist about a text, or to take some other authority's word for what is *really* important about it.

On social media, one often encounters debates about whether people — people "on the left", working-class people, both/and, whoever — really *ought* or *need* to read Marx, or whether "theory", such as it is, will always be trumped by what experience might teach you "in the real world". Well: obviously I think people should read Marx, I'm the guy whose abridgement of *The German Ideology* you're reading the Introduction to, but I suppose my take on the whole "reading Marx" thing is this: yes, everyone should probably read Marx, if they've got time. But that doesn't mean that everyone should *also* be forced to do Marx *scholarship*, at least not for themselves. To this end, I have also included a liberal array of explanatory footnotes — clarifying philosophical points, as well as doing things like "explaining who these people Marx and Engels are talking about are". I've also done things like ensuring that Latin or French terms are translated into English: I know too well, from personal experience, the frustrations that can result when you've been allowed to leave your comprehensive school only able to use French to say that you have a brother, and would like to go to the swimming pool.

I have also used the creative licence I have granted myself to do a third thing. This abridgement comprises four chapters. Chapter 1 gives my version of the "Feuerbach" chapter, so-called. Chapter 2 gives my version of the Stirner chapter. But then in Chapter 3, I provide an abridgement *of my abridgement*, boiling down my abridgement to four key sections, which can be read, either instead of the "main", "long" abridgement, or just to refresh your memory of the key points after you've read it maybe once. Then, in Chapter 4, I provide an abridgement of the abridgement of the abridgement — but that's only one sentence long.

(3)

As this edition is intended, in the first instance, for students and lay readers, it would probably be a good idea to situate *The German Ideology* in terms of Marx and Engels' lives, and their intellectual development overall.

Marx was born in Trier, near the German border with Luxembourg, in 1818; Engels was born two years later in Barmen, North Rhine-Westphalia — an industrial centre which was later merged, Stoke-on-Trent style, with a bunch of other nearby municipalities to form the city of Wuppertal. Marx's family were upper middle-class assimilated Jews: both of his parents converted to Christianity as adults, and his father, the son of a Rabbi who had been the first member of his family to receive a secular education, worked as a lawyer. A maternal uncle would go on to found the Philips electronics company — they of "PSV Eindhoven" fame. Engels' family, meanwhile, were not just simply "prosperous" but very definitely "wealthy", and owned cotton mills not only in Barmen but in Salford: Engels' radical politics would develop, in part, through his exposure to conditions at the factories his family owned, and indeed he met his partner, a working-class Irish woman named Mary Burns, on a Salford factory floor.

When Marx and Engels were young men, G.W.F. Hegel, who from 1818 until his death in 1831 had been Professor of Philosophy at the University of Berlin, was by far the dominant intellectual figure of the day. Hegel's work represents the high point of the "German Idealist" philosophy which developed in the wake of Kant's *Critique of Pure Reason* (1781). Essentially, Hegel's thought is a form of "Absolute Idealism" in which, over the course of a process of historical development, what is experienced by the mind comes to be identified *absolutely* with what actually exists in the world. In his central work of political philosophy, the *Philosophy of Right* (1820), Hegel outlined an account of the state grounded in his "reconstructive" method, in which the political system that we have right now is analysed retrospectively, as having come to be as the result of a process of rational development. In this way, we come to realise how it might be justified — or at least, how the system might justify *itself*, internally.

In the wake of his death, Hegel's followers were split between two camps: the "Old", or "Right" Hegelians, who believed history to have culminated both in Hegel's thought and in the institutions of the Prussian state which employed him, and the "Young" or "Left" Hegelians, who attempted to use Hegelian resources to develop a radical critique of existing conditions — that reconstructive method, after all, might throw up certain internal contradictions, as well as justifications. Prominent Young Hegelians included the aforementioned Ludwig Feuerbach and Bruno Bauer; Stirner, like Marx and Engels, moved in Young Hegelian circles, but ultimately came to position himself towards them as an antagonist. It was through their exposure to the Young Hegelians that Marx and Engels both came to something like philosophical maturity.

Marx moved to Berlin to study in 1836, and was still there when Engels moved to the capital in 1841. They did not meet, however, until 1842, by which time Marx had been appointed editor of a Cologne-based radical newspaper called the *Rheinische Zeitung* — Marx was barred from pursuing an academic career due to his far-left political views, and as a result of this ended up working as a journalist, off and on, throughout his adult life. Initially, the two men did not get on particularly well, but this changed in 1844, when they met in Paris, where Marx had moved after the Prussian state had closed down the *Rheinische Zeitung* — politics also interfered with his journalistic career, of course — and decided to collaborate on a manuscript critiquing the Young Hegelians called *The Holy Family*. The title "Family" were Bruno Bauer, and his brother Edgar — an anarchist who would later work for the Danish government as a police spy.

In Paris, Marx published a journal called the *Deutsch-Französische Zeitung*, which featured — among other pieces — his article "On the Jewish Question", yet another critique of Bauer. During this period, Marx also wrote the important pieces contained in the so-called "Paris Manuscripts", which were "re-discovered" at around the same time as the alleged *German Ideology* — these included his essay on "Alienated Labour", which has also gone on to become a staple of undergraduate philosophy courses on Marx.

In 1845, Marx was expelled from France by order of the Minister of the Interior — again because he was simply

Too Left Wing. This led to a move to Brussels. Belgium had only been founded in 1830, and at this point had one of the most liberal constitutions in the world — even so, Marx still had to pledge not to write anything about contemporary politics in order to be allowed to stay. Many other exiled socialists had taken refuge in Brussels, including Marx's friends Moses Hess and Joseph Weydemeyer; a couple of months after Marx arrived there, Engels decided to join them. It was at this point that they began researching and writing the manuscripts that we now know as *The German Ideology*.

Marx's Paris manuscripts are still clearly marked by the influence of Feuerbach, whose "humanist" version of materialism remains committed to the idea of some sort of immutable, historically constant, human "essence". In large part, the point of Marx and Engels' studies for *The German Ideology* was to put socialism on a genuinely scientific (as opposed to philosophical, idealist) footing — by finding a way to abandon their own residual Feuerbachian pretensions. This is the main intellectual context in which their turn towards "historical materialism" must be understood: *The German Ideology* is an attempt to regard the human animal as a creature that has emerged in and with — not outside of, and above — history.

The other major figure Marx and Engels were grappling with was, of course, Stirner. "Max Stirner" was the pen-name of Johann Kaspar Schmidt, a Berlin teacher who worked in a girl's school. Stirner, whose attempt at an academic career had ended in failure after he failed the oral component of his PhD examination, had attended meetings of the Young Hegelians in Berlin, and had been particularly close to Engels. Today, the only visual representations of Stirner we have are caricatures that Engels drew decades later at the request of Stirner's biographer, John Henry Mackay. A quiet, withdrawn man who seems to have had no genuinely close friends — even his wife later claimed to have never particularly liked him — in 1844 Stirner published a book entitled *The Ego and Its Own*, which was itself intended, at least in part, as a sweeping critique of Feuerbach. In *The Ego and Its Own*, Stirner argued that basically everything we *think* exists, or that everything we are subject to — religion, morality, the state, our status as members of something called "the human species", whatever — is the product of a mere "spook", a "wheel in the head": something essentially *alien* to us, that we only *think* is meaningful to the extent that the thought of it holds us captive. In reality, the only thing that exists is me, *myself* — and whatever happens to exercise my interest in the present (that is, my "property" — the only coherent meaning that "property" can be even said to have at all). Beyond this, there is nothing ("I have set my cause," Stirner declares in the opening lines of the book, "on *nothing*."). *Nothing*, therefore, has any "real" value: we should all have the strength to act as consistent egoists — which is to say, as nihilists.

Such a work, of course, might *prima facie* sound so wildly opposed to Marx and Engels' communist views that they would really be perfectly justified in never bothering to refute it. But in fact, Marx and Engels found Stirner fascinating. Engels, in particular, was highly enthused by Stirner's book when he first read it — in part because Stirner's criticisms of the Young Hegelian tradition were in a way so similar to the ones he was at that point in the process of developing in association with Marx. Indeed, in a letter to Marx dated 19 November 1844, Engels even wrote that Stirner's Egoism "is taken to such a pitch, it is so absurd and at the same time so self-aware, that it cannot maintain itself even for an instant in its one-sidedness, but must immediately change into Communism." Marx's initial reply to this letter has been lost, but other letters suggest that he was far less taken with the work, indeed that he rather poured cold water on Engels' gushing reception of it — but even he was influenced enough by it to assist with the production of over 300 pages of very detailed close-reading and critique. Again, there is a bit of a caveat here, because the "Stirner" manuscript is, aside from being very detailed, also singularly uncharitable to its opponent: Marx is often a very funny writer, but here the insults typically have a chortling, schoolboy tone — and also don't really make that much sense unless you know both your Young Hegelians, and your *Don Quixote*... there is a <u>lot</u> in the Stirner chapter about *Don Quixote*.

In essence though, the Stirner section is important because it helps clarify what Marx and Engels take to be the relation between individual and class interest, and how this means that, with a critical mass of the population having been proletarianised by capitalism, the abolition of class society will inevitably result. In short: if people really *are* as bourgeois society takes them to be — self-interested individuals — then eventually it will be in the egoistic interest of enough individuals to band together to overthrow the system which works *against* their interests. Although with *this*, of course, the basis of egoistic 'individualism', as we presently know it, will be abolished. The advantage of this account is that it allows us to understand the individual as a historical category, while also showing that communism can be brought about, as it were, *extra-morally*, entirely in line with the disenchanted behavioural assumptions of capitalist economists: only through the actions of selfish people, who never need to anything other than act selfishly.

Though Marx and Engels would ultimately leave *The German Ideology* both unpublished and incomplete, the work nevertheless played a central role in their intellectual development. Marx later wrote of using the work he did towards *The German Ideology* to, in a way, *purge* himself of the strictures of the academic philosophy of his day. In my view, he remained a philosopher, even after it — or at any rate, he continued to *think philosophically*, to use philosophical resources to analyse and criticise the world. But he was no longer — and this is crucial — engaged in anything like the pursuit of philosophy *for its own sake*. Rather, what we see after *The German Ideology* is what Marx himself said he got out of working on it: a Marx *liberated* from his "erstwhile philosophical conscience", and thus able to reflect on the world in much more varied, active, transformative ways — with no pedantic academic superego constantly looking over his shoulder; no revered philosophical mentors to feel like he was having to be "true" to. The results of this were first seen in *The Communist Manifesto* (1848), before condensing into the project that would consume Marx's activities for almost the whole of the rest of his life — his "Economics", the work which would later become *Capital* (*Vol. 1*, published 1867).

(4)

The German Ideology was thus essentially a project that Marx and Engels undertook at a moment of transition: a sort of evolutionary bottleneck into which they threw all the philosophy, radical or otherwise, that they had been raised on — with something quite different being thrown out, like the coloured beams of light that emerge from a prism, at the other end.

But *The German Ideology* is also the *culmination* of something: it represents the culmination — and should really be seen I think as the *overcoming* — of the German Idealist tradition in philosophy. Roughly, the story of German Idealism is as follows: in 1739, a book called *A Treatise of Human Nature* was published, whose author was a melancholy young Scottish philosopher named David

Hume. The *Treatise* was far from an instant success; Hume later complained that it "fell dead-born from the presses". But in time, it picked up a substantial following — not least as a result of the unsettling radicalism of its message. Hume was an Empiricist, but he was also a sceptic: proceeding consistently from experience, Hume argued that we have almost no reason to believe that any of the things we *think* we know about things like how the world is casually structured, or the existence of the self over time, are real.

But the point of Hume's work wasn't really to declare the entire world, and ourselves, non-existent. The point, rather, was to establish that we have no *rational* grounds for believing in them. "Most fortunately it happens," Hume declares towards the end of Book 1 of his *Treatise*:

> that since reason is incapable of dispelling these clouds, nature herself suffices to that purpose, and cures me of this philosophical melancholy and delirium, either by relaxing this bent of mind, or by some avocation, and lively impression of my senses, which obliterate all these chimeras. I dine, I play a game of back-gammon, I converse, and am merry with my friends; and when after three or four hour's amusement, I wou'd return to these speculations, they appear so cold, and strain'd, and ridiculous, that I cannot find in my heart to enter into them any farther.

Hume's work was thus not an attack on "reality", such as it is, but rather a rebuttal to the pretensions of reason — in particular, those of the "Rationalist" philosophy that was the chief rival to Empiricism in its day; dominant in Germany through the school of Gottfried Leibniz and his chief successor Christian Wolff. In Hume's vision, Rationalist metaphysics — which was deduced from a number of basic premises, carried over from Ancient and Scholastic philosophy, such as the Principle of Non-Contradiction ("it cannot happen that the same thing both is and is not") and the Principle of Sufficient Reason ("everything has a cause") — was in truth little more than idle speculation. As Hume put it: "reason is the slave of the passions" — a nice little reflective gloss on our largely blind, hungry, all-too-finite whims. Nothing is ever finally, definitely certain — and all high philosophising is bunk.

Now, of course, all this Scottish Empiricist scepticism might never have eventually mutated into something called "German Idealism" — if it wasn't for the fact that in 1724, in the Baltic city of Königsberg, not long replaced by Berlin as the capital of Prussia, a man named Immanuel Kant had been born. Kant lived in Königsberg his whole life, studying at the university there before later being named Professor of Logic and Metaphysics. Kant had been raised a faithful student of the Rationalist school — although he was always a somewhat heterodox member, very into his Newtonian physics, and as up as he could be on recent developments in the physical sciences. And then, at some point, around 1770, Kant was exposed to the ideas of Hume. It's unclear if Kant actually read Hume directly: Kant did not read English, and a full translation of the *Treatise* was only published in 1790; although other Hume texts were available in German, and parts of the *Treatise* had been translated much earlier by Kant's neighbour — and uncanny intellectual double — J.G. Hamann, a crochety anti-Enlightenment mystic who studied philosophy while skiving off from his job in the Königsberg customs office. However the exposure happened though, its effect was profound: in later work, Kant wrote of being shaken awake, by Hume, from the "dogmatic slumber" that he had previously found himself snoozing comfortably in. Nothing about Hume's ideas would allow Kant to rest easy: his scepticism threw every intellectual certainty that Kant had been raised on into flux.

And the reason why Kant is so important a philosopher is that eventually, over the course of his so-called "silent decade", between the ages of 45 and 55, during which, in contemplation of Hume, he published nothing, he found a way to look his demon in the eye — and, arguably, defeat him. Kant realised that Hume's arguments demolished the Rationalist philosophy that he knew. But he could not accept Hume's conclusion: that things like the Law of Causality are merely the result of "nature" or "habit" — that we have no rational grounds on which to affirm them; that they might in a way be discarded at any point, subject to our whims.

In his landmark work, *The Critique of Pure Reason* (1781), Kant presents the case for the validity of metaphysical categories like Causality or Substance as being what he calls synthetic *a priori* — unalterably necessary conditions on the possibility of any experience. Without the things that Hume says we have no rational grounds for believing in, then, no experience of the world — even an illusory one — could possibly take place. Kant thus salvages the vestiges of Rationalist metaphysics — by placing metaphysics on what he argues are solid, empirical grounds.

At the heart of Kant's approach to metaphysics is his doctrine of "transcendental idealism". Philosophical "realism" holds that the world exists independently of our experience of it; "idealism", by contrast, identifies our experience with reality as such. "Transcendental idealism" is a classic third-way position: through it, Kant is able to hold that the "empirically real" world — the world as we experience it — is just how it *appears* under the categories, which, he argues, have been brought to bear on it by us. In this way, Kant's idealism is intended as a way of securing a consistent, empirical realism.

Beautiful, in a way — but one is only able to adopt transcendental idealism at great metaphysical cost. For while Kant's doctrine allows us to talk about the world we experience as being, in a way, "real", it also instantiates an irresolvable dualism: between this "empirically real" world of "appearances", and the world as it is "in-itself" — how reality *would* be, if we were able to process it shorn off and separate from how we both intuit and understand it. The image of this ultimate, unknowable, extra-real reality haunts Kant's system: the loose bit of electrical tape with which he has attempted to bind his system together, fraying at the bottom of the world.

Kant's work was hugely successful in his lifetime: by the beginning of the 1790s, the *Critique of Pure Reason* had radically transformed the German philosophical scene. Practically all the exciting young philosophers in the German states were self-consciously "Kantian" in some way — and yet almost all of them were working on some way to overcome transcendental idealism. As the influential post-Kantian philosopher F.H. Jacobi once quipped: "Without the proposition of the thing-in-itself, I was unable to enter Kant's system — with it, I was unable to stay."

The dialectic of philosophy in the immediate wake of Kant ran something like this. The first really monumental successor to Kant was a man named J.G. Fichte. Fichte saw himself as radicalising Kant's system: going beyond Kant to produce a philosophy even more Kantian than Kant's own. Fichte's radicalisation proceeds from the thought that we don't really need to have anything to do with the thing in-itself, because really everything is in some sense grounded in the free activity of the subject, the "I". Fichte, understandably, has often been accused of thinking that we just sort of create the world — that it is a product of our imaginations — but that's not really the case at all. Rather, he is a thinker of the radical Enlightenment, who emphasises the endless, practical striving of free, rational subjects to dominate irrational nature and bend it to their wills — a vision, in fact, that is carried over in no small way into the Promethean elements of Marx's thought: the idea of "conscious mastery", for instance, that we will read Marx and Engels discussing in the main text below.

At the height of his fame, Fichte lectured in Jena, by this point the most important intellectual centre of the German-speaking world. During this period, his most obviously brilliant disciple was an ambitious young philosopher named Friedrich Wilhelm Joseph Schelling, who would work to take post-Kantian philosophy in a quite different direction. Whereas Fichte attempted to overcome the doctrine of thing in-itself by eliminating it, Schelling did so by incorporating it into his story of how the thinking subject has come to exist at all: for Schelling, what Fichte thought of as "nature" —the "not-I" is *what gives rise* to the (Fichtean) "I", which then finds itself in a position to make sense of it. Schelling's work can be hard to summarise, because he kept subjecting his system to various sweeping revisions throughout his career — so quite possibly none of the terminology I've used here is technically consistent or, relative to any of Schelling's actual works, correct. But at its core is some sort of insistence of the *identity* of the subject with the object. It is usually noted at this point that Schelling's work was deeply influenced by that of Spinoza, whose Rationalist pantheism had been proscribed as a form of atheism.

So really what we have here is two strategies for overcoming transcendental idealism: one "subjectivist" — a strategy which leads to a more radical and bombastic form of idealism; the other "objectivist" — and which seems really to lead back to a form of Rationalism. Ultimately, these approaches were synthesised, in typically Hegelian style, by Hegel — who had been Schelling's room-mate when they studied together at seminarial college, and who struggled in his shadow for years before eventually triumphantly surpassing him. Hegel's innovation was to conceive of history as a "dialectical" process through which Spirit ("reason", "mind", "consciousness", whatever you want to call it) becomes aware of itself — which is the same as to say that this is how said Spirit becomes aware of what there "really" is in the world. In this way, Hegel's system represents the baking of a Kantian cake that we are able to eat too: the world "really" is how it appears to us, and this world "really" is the world — because we are able to show, citing a process of rational development — a process which proceeds, incidentally, from absolutely no dogmatic principles whatsoever — that the ways in which we experience it are (also) objectively valid.

As noted above: in his own time, Hegel's thought was often considered to be the final culmination of "philosophy" as a whole. While much less widespread nowadays, this view does still have at least some adherents, and certainly Hegel continues to be a philosophical giant — a pretty well unavoidable subject of study in the history of philosophy, even in the analytic philosophy departments whose outlook was in many ways founded on the rejection of Hegel effected by Bertrand Russell and G.E. Moore. And yet: for all Hegel's system might seem, on paper, to be magnificently convincing, there nevertheless remains something about it that can feel naggingly unsatisfactory. Many important philosophical figures have been defined by their basic disenchantment with Hegel — not just the early analytics and certain of the Young Hegelians, but also the likes of Schopenhauer and Kierkegaard, as well as (of course) Marx.

For me, the source of this dissatisfaction can be expressed in the following way: Hegel's achievement was to provide the solution to a certain Kantian problematic. Kant's achievement was to salvage Rationalist metaphysics from the tradition's savaging by Hume, while simultaneously saving Hume's own consistent Empiricism from the skeptical demon. But then he left us with transcendental idealism, which is a doctrine no one really likes: very few philosophers are able to see a dualism they don't immediately want to overcome. Hegel solves that Kantian problem by making Reason — as Spirit — *absolute*. And this, in a way, means that he undermines something vital about Kant's response to Hume. In Kant, there remains space for reason's opposite — the claims of which *Hume* is really all about. But in Hegel, that space ends up getting eliminated. At the end of the dialectical day, there is no more tarrying with the irrational. And this is more than a little bit unfortunate. Because there are all sorts of things that the irrational is *good* for.

Kierkegaard, for instance, believed that Hegel had effectively eliminated any space for faith in God, the "religious" stage or sphere or experience through which all things — whether "rational" or otherwise — are possible. For Schopenhauer, meanwhile, it meant that Hegel had deliberately blinded himself to what he — Schopenhauer — identified with the Kantian world in-itself: namely "The Will", an endless, ever-same and inhuman process of blind, instinctual striving. Personally, my big problem with Hegel is that, in making Reason absolute, he turns it into something that is, essentially, sovereign over individuals: Reason, for instance, is for the Hegelian supposed to be embedded in our political "institutions", as they have developed over time. But this can end up leading to some bizarre intellectual manoeuvres: Adorno, for instance, relates in one of his lectures a story about the Hegelian Marxist György Lukács, who after an argument with his (Communist) party, told Adorno that "the party was in the right... because it embodied the objective state of history" — even if, Lukács felt, "his ideas and arguments were better than the party's". Obviously one might sometimes really just be being (stupidly) wilful. But surely if your experience and insight is telling you one thing, but some relevant institution maintains the opposite... there has to be *something* to settle the matter; something beyond just "this is what the institution happens to maintain"? Something beyond Reason, perhaps, that has helped form Reason – made it how it is?

There is good reason, then, to push the dialectic of philosophy past Hegel — and that means going, I think, somehow back to Hume. We can think of this in terms of a basic question, which Hume seems to be asking: "Why is anything the way that we say, or think, it is?" Hume's answer is: "There is no reason. It's just nature, or habit." Kant's is: "Because experience is grounded in certain things which could not be otherwise (or experience wouldn't be possible)." Hegel's is: "That's right Kant. And also we know those things are absolutely valid, because of History." And it is at this point that the gears in Marx's head start turning. From some distant corner of this philosophical room, Max Stirner, sat next to the Young Hegelians, mostly silent, declares: "But actually, everything *could* be different. We could just *say* that it was different if we wanted to." Most people in the room are thinking: "Urgh, shut up, Stirner." But Marx is thinking: "Why don't we think that everything is different? What has *actually* made everything the way that it is? It can't just be this absolutely rational Spirit thing, unfolding itself inside-out. There has to be some *reason*, in short, for Spirit to have developed as it has." Something extra-rational — which we can then use to lever a critique of Reason as such.

This, at any rate, is what Marx and Engels give us in *The German Ideology*. Their materialist philosophy of history pushes past Hegel and back to Hume, because it helps us understand how this basically irrational thing — "human nature", the sum of our crudest appetitive drives — has produced society as we know it today, and may yet one day manage to yield something better. They take their cues, as they tell us, from human beings as they are — "real", and "active" — and show us how these selfish, irrational, needing and desiring things may one day bring about a world they are able to exercise "conscious mastery" over, and be free in relation towards — preserving what remains of a very distinctively German Idealist longing for "autonomy". In *The German Ideology*, Marx and Engels overcome Hegel, by placing Spirit firmly on its stomach.

(5)

Here, at any rate, is my reading of the text. In my view, what *The German Ideology* allows us to do, is to *dissolve* a certain historical tendency in the history of philosophy, towards the construction of the sorts of philosophical "systems" that philosophers working in the German tradition they emerged from were typically given to try and build. The Idealist tradition constructs elaborate solutions to internal problems thrown up by reflection on Reason — and ends up crowning Reason as sovereign. Marx and Engels, by contrast, consider philosophical problems, such as they are, as always already reflections of material conflicts in the world. Their solution must thus be sought not in abstract system-building, but in "real-world" practice: thought must strive not simply to *understand* the world but — as Marx would put this point in his famous twelfth "Thesis on Feuerbach" — to *change* it.

In my view, then, what *The German Ideology* is really doing is presenting historical materialism as a sort of "philosophical therapy" — an approach more usually associated with Wittgenstein and his disciples (although arguably this is also what is going on in the much more obviously Marxist tradition of critical theory). For

Wittgenstein, most if not all philosophical problems are the result of some sort of linguistic puzzlement or confusion: one only has to clear that little muddle up, and there is no need for any "heavy duty", "constructive" philosophy at all. Marx and Engels are doing something similar, only they don't think that the philosophical tradition is the result of a bunch of armchair mishaps to do with *language*: what they show us is that it has formed as the reflection, throughout history, of various material inequalities and struggles for power. As I already noted in section 1 of this Introduction above, this represents in my view a new "way of seeing" — a perspective from which a lot of the particular logical moves of the Idealist tradition can not only be understood as the reflection of "ruling-class ideology" or whatever, but simply, pragmatically, dissolved. It is in this sense that *The German Ideology* represents, as I have said, both the "culmination" and the "overcoming" of this tradition in philosophy: remedying its tendency towards scholasticism, while realising — a lot more definitively — the practical impetus which had always motivated thinkers like Fichte.

The German Ideology remains a vitally important text, because it provides us with a philosophical method that leaves us free to think about the world in an active, transformative way — which turns philosophy, really, *into* this sort of active, transformative thinking. This "way of seeing", as I've called it, is thus of particular importance for radical, emancipatory political movements — of the sort that Marx and Engels both have inspired, in various ways, and continue to inspire today. And probably always will inspire — just so long as the poor are exploited and the world remains essentially Bad. I hope my abridgement helps both to communicate, and make sense of, those lessons.

THE GERMAN IDEOLOGY

A NEW ABRIDGEMENT

Karl Marx
and
Friedrich Engels

PREFACE

Hitherto men have constantly made up for themselves false conceptions about themselves, about what they are and what they ought to be. They have arranged their relationships according to their ideas of God, of normal man, etc. The phantoms of their brains have got out of their hands. They, the creators, have bowed down before their creations. Let us liberate them from the chimeras, the ideas, dogmas, imaginary beings under the yoke of which they are pining away. Let us revolt against the rule of thoughts. Let us teach men, says one, to exchange these imaginations for thoughts which correspond to the essence of man; says the second, to take up a critical attitude to them; says the third, to knock them out of their heads; and — existing reality will collapse.[1]

These innocent and childlike fancies are the kernel of the modern Young Hegelian philosophy, which not only is received by the German public with horror and awe, but is announced by our philosophic heroes with the solemn consciousness of its cataclysmic dangerousness and criminal

---

1 The three thinkers hinted at here are Ludwig Feuerbach (1804-1872), Bruno Bauer (1809-1882), and Johann Kaspar Schmidt *aka* Max Stirner (1806-1856). Ostensibly, *The German Ideology* — or, the first volume of it, as Marx and Engels specify below — critiques each of these thinkers in turn. See my Introduction for why this isn't really true.

ruthlessness.[2] The first volume of the present publication has the aim of uncloaking these sheep, who take themselves and are taken for wolves; of showing how their bleating merely imitates in a philosophic form the conceptions of the German middle class; how the boasting of these philosophic commentators only mirrors the wretchedness of the real conditions in Germany. It is its aim to debunk and discredit the philosophic struggle with the shadows of reality, which appeals to the dreamy and muddled German nation.

Once upon a time a valiant fellow had the idea that men were drowned in water only because they were possessed with the *idea of gravity*. If they were to knock this notion out of their heads, say by stating it to be a superstition, a religious concept, they would be sublimely proof against any danger from water. His whole life long he fought against the illusion of gravity, of whose harmful results all statistics brought him new and manifold evidence. This valiant fellow was the type of the new revolutionary philosophers in Germany.

---

2 The Young Hegelians emerged in the wake of the death of G.W.F. Hegel (1770-1831), a monumental figure whose work continues to shape Western thought. For more on the Young Hegelians, and philosophy both immediately prior to, and in the wake of, Hegel, see my Introduction.

1. "THE CHAPTER ON FEUERBACH" OR: "SOME NOTES WHICH AREN'T ACTUALLY ON FEUERBACH, BUT WHICH WERE AT ONE STAGE FUDGED INTO A CHAPTER CALLED 'FEUERBACH'", OR: "MATERIALISM AS PHILOSOPHICAL THERAPY: TOWARDS THE CONSTANT OVERTHROW OF ALL EXISTING STATES OF AFFAIRS"

A. Idealism and Materialism

The Illusions of German Ideology

As we hear from German ideologists, Germany has in the last few years gone through an unparalleled revolution. The decomposition of the Hegelian philosophy, which began with Strauss,[3] has developed into a universal ferment into which all the "powers of the past" are swept. In the general chaos mighty empires have arisen only to meet with immediate doom, heroes have emerged momentarily only to be hurled back into obscurity by bolder and stronger rivals. It was a revolution beside which the French Revolution was child's play, a world struggle beside which the struggles of

---

3 David Strauss (1808-1874). His critical *Life of Jesus* (1835-36) made the then deeply controversial distinction between the real, historical Jesus, and the miracle-working figures described in the New Testament — and drew him into conflict with Hegelians like Bauer. And not just them, either: the Earl of Shaftesbury described it as "the most pestilential book ever vomited out of the jaws of hell".

the Diadochi[4] appear insignificant. Principles ousted one another, heroes of the mind overthrew each other with unheard-of rapidity, and in the three years 1842-45 more of the past was swept away in Germany than at other times in three centuries.

All this is supposed to have taken place in the realm of pure thought.

Certainly it is an interesting event we are dealing with: the putrescence of the absolute spirit. When the last spark of its life had failed, the various components of this *caput mortuum* began to decompose, entered into new combinations and formed new substances. The industrialists of philosophy, who till then had lived on the exploitation of the absolute spirit, now seized upon the new combinations. Each with all possible zeal set about retailing his apportioned share. This naturally gave rise to competition, which, to start with, was carried on in moderately staid bourgeois fashion. Later when the German market was glutted, and the commodity in spite of all efforts found no response in the world market, the business was spoiled in the usual German manner by fabricated and fictitious production, deterioration in quality, adulteration of the raw materials, falsification of labels, fictitious purchases, bill-jobbing and a credit system devoid of any real basis.[5] The competition turned into a bitter struggle, which is now being extolled and interpreted

---

4 The rival generals who fought over the remnants of Alexander's empire following his death.

5 Marx and Engels were writing in a context when Germany, not yet politically united, was still considered very economically backward. Perhaps this is why their ideas feel so relevant to me, a British person, in 2021: they are writing for people who come from a place that sucks.

to us as a revolution of world significance, the begetter of the most prodigious results and achievements.

If we wish to rate at its true value this philosophic charlatanry, which awakens even in the breast of the honest German citizen a glow of national pride, if we wish to bring out clearly the pettiness, the parochial narrowness of this whole Young Hegelian movement and in particular the tragicomic contrast between the illusions of these heroes about their achievements and the actual achievements themselves, we must look at the whole spectacle from a standpoint beyond the frontiers of Germany.

German criticism has, right up to its latest efforts, never quitted the realm of philosophy. Far from examining its general philosophic premises, the whole body of its inquiries has actually sprung from the soil of a definite philosophical system, that of Hegel. Not only in their answers but in their very questions there was a mystification. This dependence on Hegel is the reason why not one of these modern critics has even attempted a comprehensive criticism of the Hegelian system, however much each professes to have advanced beyond Hegel. Their polemics against Hegel and against one another are confined to this: each extracts one side of the Hegelian system and turns this against the whole system as well as against the sides extracted by the others. To begin with they extracted pure unfalsified Hegelian categories such as "substance" and "self-consciousness", later they desecrated these categories with more secular names such as "species", "the Unique", "Man", etc.

The entire body of German philosophical criticism from Strauss to Stirner is confined to criticism of religious conceptions. The critics started from real religion and actual theology.[6] What religious consciousness and a religious conception really meant was determined variously

---

6 As Strauss did; as Feuerbach did.

as they went along. Their advance consisted in subsuming the allegedly dominant metaphysical, political, juridical, moral and other conceptions under the class of religious or theological conceptions; and similarly in pronouncing political, juridical, moral consciousness as religious or theological, and the political, juridical, moral man — "*man*" in the last resort — as religious. The dominance of religion was taken for granted. Gradually every dominant relationship was pronounced a religious relationship and transformed into a cult, a cult of law, a cult of the State, etc. On all sides it was only a question of dogmas and belief in dogmas. The world was sanctified to an ever-increasing extent till at last our venerable Saint Max was able to canonise it *en bloc* and thus dispose of it once for all.

The Old Hegelians had *comprehended* everything as soon as it was reduced to an Hegelian logical category. The Young Hegelians *criticised* everything by attributing to it religious conceptions or by pronouncing it a theological matter. The Young Hegelians are in agreement with the Old Hegelians in their belief in the rule of religion, of concepts, of a universal principle in the existing world. Only, the one party attacks this dominion as usurpation, while the other extols it as legitimate.[7]

Since the Young Hegelians consider conceptions, thoughts, ideas, in fact all the products of consciousness, to which they attribute an independent existence, as the

---

7 This point remains apt to this day: "radical" academic philosophy, such as it is, remains by and large a "Young Hegelian" sort of thing, trapped by its own moralistic abstractions. And actually, the point might be extended well beyond the reasons why people like me and my friends suck. What else are campaigns to "raise awareness" of some given condition or state of affairs, if not a "Young Hegelian"-style criticism of reality, mistaking the defeat of something in practice, for its vanquishing in the arena of ideas?

real chains of men (just as the Old Hegelians declared them the true bonds of human society) it is evident that the Young Hegelians have to fight only against these illusions of consciousness. Since, according to their fantasy, the relationships of men, all their doings, their chains and their limitations are products of their consciousness, the Young Hegelians logically put to men the moral postulate of exchanging their present consciousness for human, critical or egoistic consciousness, and thus of removing their limitations.

This demand to change consciousness amounts to a demand to interpret reality in another way, i.e. to recognise it by means of another interpretation.[8] The Young Hegelian ideologists, in spite of their allegedly "world-shattering" statements, are the staunchest conservatives. The most recent of them have found the correct expression for their activity when they declare they are only fighting against "*phrases*". They forget, however, that to these phrases they themselves are only opposing other phrases, and that they are in no way combating the real existing world when they are merely combating the phrases of this world. The only results which this philosophic criticism could achieve were a few (and at that thoroughly one-sided) elucidations of Christianity from the point of view of religious history; all the rest of their assertions are only further embellishments of their claim to have furnished, in these unimportant elucidations, discoveries of universal importance. It has not occurred to any one of these

---

8 There are echoes here of Marx's twelfth thesis on Feuerbach (the "Theses on Feuerbach", incidentally, are much more obviously to do with Feuerbach than anything in the "Feuerbach" chapter of *The German Ideology*): "The philosophers have only interpreted the world, in various ways; the point is to change it." (See chapter 4 of this edition.)

philosophers to inquire into the connection of German philosophy with German reality, the relation of their criticism to their own material surroundings.

First Premises of Materialist Method

The premises from which we begin are not arbitrary ones, not dogmas, but real premises from which abstraction can only be made in the imagination. They are the real individuals, their activity and the material conditions of their life, both those which they find already existing and those produced by their activity. These premises can thus be verified in a purely empirical way.

The first premise of all human history is, of course, the existence of living human individuals. Thus the first fact to be established is the physical organisation of these individuals and their consequent relation to the rest of nature. Of course, we cannot here go either into the actual physical nature of man, or into the natural conditions in which man finds himself — geological, hydrographical,[9] climatic and so on. All historical writing must set out from these natural bases and their modification in the course of history through the action of men.

Men can be distinguished from animals by consciousness, by religion or anything else you like.[10] They themselves begin

---

9 From the dictionary: "a branch of hydrography that deals with the relations of mountains to drainage".

10 Interestingly, in his earlier essay on "Alienated Labour" (from the so-called *Economic and Philosophical Manuscripts of 1844*), Marx writes that: "The animal only fashions things according to the standards and needs of the species it belongs to, whereas man knows how to produce according to the measure of every species and knows everywhere how to apply its inherent standard to the object; thus man also fashions things according

to distinguish themselves from animals as soon as they begin to produce their means of subsistence, a step which is conditioned by their physical organisation. By producing their means of subsistence men are indirectly producing their material life. The way in which men produce their means of subsistence depends first of all on the nature of the means of subsistence they actually find in existence and have to reproduce. This mode of production must not be considered simply as being the reproduction of the physical existence of the individuals. Rather it is a definite form of activity of these individuals, a definite form of expressing their life, a definite mode of life on their part. As individuals express their life, so they are. What they are, therefore, coincides with their production, both with what they produce and with *how* they produce. Hence what individuals are depends on the material conditions of their production. This production only makes its appearance with the increase of population. In its turn this presupposes the *intercourse* of individuals with one another. The form of this intercourse is again determined by production.

The relations of different nations among themselves depend upon the extent to which each has developed its productive forces, the division of labour and internal

---

to the laws of beauty." In short: for the (slightly) earlier Marx, "man" remains an essentially Idealist creature, distinguished by His resonance with some heavenly "inherent standard". There is a clear progression from and overcoming of that earlier view here. I owe to Dan Swain the suggestion that I also cite this line from the section of vol. II of *The German Ideology* on the "True Socialist" writer Karl Grün: "Anyway, what sort of man is this, 'man' who is not seen in his real historical activity and existence, but can be deduced from the lobe of his own ear or from some other feature which distinguishes him from the animals? Such a man 'is contained' in himself, like his own pimple."

intercourse. This statement is generally recognised. But not only the relation of one nation to others, but also the whole internal structure of the nation itself depends on the stage of development reached by its production and its internal and external intercourse. How far the productive forces of a nation are developed is shown most manifestly by the degree to which the division of labour has been carried. Each new productive force, insofar as it is not merely a quantitative extension of productive forces already known (for instance the bringing into cultivation of fresh land), causes a further development of the division of labour.

The division of labour inside a nation leads at first to the separation of industrial and commercial from agricultural labour, and hence to the separation of *town* and *country* and to the conflict of their interests. Its further development leads to the separation of commercial from industrial labour. At the same time through the division of labour inside these various branches there develop various divisions among the individuals co-operating in definite kinds of labour. The relative position of these individual groups is determined by the methods employed in agriculture, industry and commerce (patriarchalism, slavery, estates, classes). These same conditions are to be seen (given a more developed intercourse) in the relations of different nations to one another.

The various stages of development in the division of labour are just so many different forms of ownership, i.e. the existing stage in the division of labour determines also the relations of individuals to one another with reference to the material, instrument, and product of labour.

The first form of ownership is tribal ownership. It corresponds to the undeveloped stage of production, at which a people lives by hunting and fishing, by the rearing of beasts or, in the highest stage, agriculture. In the latter case it presupposes a great mass of uncultivated stretches of land. The division of labour is at this stage still very elementary and is confined to a further extension of the natural division of labour existing in the family. The social structure is, therefore, limited to an extension of the family; patriarchal family chieftains, below them the members of the tribe, finally slaves. The slavery latent in the family only develops gradually with the increase of population, the growth of wants, and with the extension of external relations, both of war and of barter.

The second form is the ancient communal and State ownership which proceeds especially from the union of several tribes into a city by agreement or by conquest, and which is still accompanied by slavery. Beside communal ownership we already find movable, and later also immovable, private property developing, but as an abnormal form subordinate to communal ownership. The citizens hold power over their labouring slaves only in their community, and on this account alone, therefore, they are bound to the form of communal ownership. It is the communal private property which compels the active citizens to remain in this spontaneously derived form of association over against their slaves. For this reason the whole structure of society based on this communal ownership, and with it the power of the people, decays in the same measure as, in particular, immovable private property evolves. The division of labour is already more developed. We already find the antagonism of town and country; later the antagonism between those states which represent town interests and those which represent country interests, and inside the towns themselves the antagonism between industry and maritime commerce. The class relation between citizens and slaves is now completely developed.

With the development of private property, we find here for the first time the same conditions which we shall find again, only on a more extensive scale, with modern private property. On the one hand, the concentration of private property, which began very early in Rome (as the Licinian agrarian law proves[11]) and proceeded very rapidly from the time of the civil wars and especially under the Emperors; on the other hand, coupled with this, the transformation of the plebeian small peasantry into a proletariat, which, however, owing to its intermediate position between propertied citizens and slaves, never achieved an independent development.

The third form of ownership is feudal or estate property. If antiquity started out from the *town* and its little territory, the Middle Ages started out from the *country*. This different starting-point was determined by the sparseness of the population at that time, which was scattered over a large area and which received no large increase from the conquerors. In contrast to Greece and Rome, feudal development at the outset, therefore, extends over a much wider territory, prepared by the Roman conquests and the spread of agriculture at first associated with it. The last centuries of the declining Roman Empire and its conquest by the barbarians destroyed a number of productive forces; agriculture had declined, industry had decayed for want of a market, trade had died out or been violently suspended, the rural and urban population had decreased. From these conditions and the mode of organisation of the conquest determined by them, feudal property developed under the influence of the Germanic military constitution. Like tribal and communal ownership, it is based again on a community; but the directly producing class standing over against it is not, as in the case of the ancient community, the slaves, but the enserfed small peasantry. As soon as feudalism is fully

---

11 A law passed in 367 BC following a struggle between the plebeians and the patriarchians. The law limited Roman citizens to holding the equivalent of 309 acres of common land.

developed, there also arises antagonism to the towns.[12] The hierarchical structure of land ownership, and the armed bodies of retainers associated with it, gave the nobility power over the serfs. This feudal organisation was, just as much as the ancient communal ownership, an association against a subjected producing class; but the form of association and the relation to the direct producers were different because of the different conditions of production.

This feudal system of land ownership had its counterpart in the *towns* in the shape of corporative property, the feudal organisation of trades. Here property consisted chiefly in the labour of each individual person. The necessity for association against the organised robber-nobility, the need for communal covered markets in an age when the industrialist was at the same time a merchant, the growing competition of the escaped serfs swarming into the rising towns, the feudal structure of the whole country: these combined to bring about the *guilds*. The gradually accumulated small capital of individual craftsmen and their stable numbers, as against the growing population, evolved the relation of journeyman and apprentice, which brought into being in the towns a hierarchy similar to that in the country.

Thus the chief form of property during the feudal epoch consisted on the one hand of landed property with serf labour chained to it, and on the other of the labour of the individual with small capital commanding the labour of journeymen. The organisation of both was determined by the restricted conditions of production — the small-scale and primitive cultivation of the land, and the craft type of industry. There was little division of labour in the heyday of feudalism. Each country bore in itself the antithesis of town and country; the division into estates was certainly

12 Lisa Nandy, take note.

strongly marked; but apart from the differentiation of princes, nobility, clergy and peasants in the country, and masters, journeymen, apprentices and soon also the rabble of casual labourers in the towns, no division of importance took place. In agriculture it was rendered difficult by the strip-system, beside which the cottage industry of the peasants themselves emerged. In industry there was no division of labour at all in the individual trades themselves, and very little between them. The separation of industry and commerce was found already in existence in older towns; in the newer it only developed later, when the towns entered into mutual relations.

The grouping of larger territories into feudal kingdoms was a necessity for the landed nobility as for the towns. The organisation of the ruling class, the nobility, had, therefore, everywhere a monarch at its head.

The fact is, therefore, that definite individuals who are productively active in a definite way enter into these definite social and political relations. Empirical observation must in each separate instance bring out empirically, and without any mystification and speculation, the connection of the social and political structure with production. The social structure and the State are continually evolving out of the life-process of definite individuals, but of individuals, not as they may appear in their own or other people's imagination, but as they *really* are — i.e. as they operate, produce materially, and hence as they work under definite material limits, presuppositions and conditions independent of their will.

The production of ideas, of conceptions, of consciousness, is at first directly interwoven with the material activity and the material intercourse of men, the language of real life. Conceiving, thinking, the mental intercourse of men, appear at this stage as the direct efflux of their material behaviour. The same applies to mental production as expressed in the language of politics, laws, morality, religion, metaphysics, etc. of a people. Men are the producers of their conceptions, ideas, etc. — real, active men, as they are conditioned by a definite development of their productive forces and of the intercourse corresponding to these, up to its furthest forms. Consciousness can never be anything else than conscious existence, and the existence of men is their actual life-process. If in all ideology men and their circumstances appear upside-down as in a *camera obscura*, this phenomenon arises just as much from their historical life-process as the inversion of objects on the retina does from their physical life-process.[13]

In direct contrast to German philosophy which descends from heaven to earth, here we ascend from earth to heaven. That is to say, we do not set out from what men say, imagine, conceive, nor from men as narrated, thought of, imagined, conceived, in order to arrive at men in the flesh. We set out from real, active men, and on the basis of their real life-process we demonstrate the development of the ideological reflexes and echoes of this life-process. The phantoms formed in the human brain are also, necessarily, sublimates of their material life-process, which is empirically verifiable and bound to material premises. Morality, religion, metaphysics, all the rest of ideology and their corresponding forms of consciousness, thus no longer retain the semblance of independence. They have no history, no development; but men, developing their material production and their material intercourse, alter, along with this their real existence, their thinking and

---

13 In this paragraph we find the central statement of historical materialism — almost a manifesto for it, really. If anything is axiomatic for Marxism, it is this. We think as we eat, shit, fuck, love, want — and our thinking is driven by such things. There is no heaven of ideas. (For more on this, see my Introduction.)

the products of their thinking. Life is not determined by consciousness, but consciousness by life. In the first method of approach the starting-point is consciousness taken as the living individual; in the second method, which conforms to real life, it is the real living individuals themselves, and consciousness is considered solely as *their* consciousness.

This method of approach is not devoid of premises. It starts out from the real premises and does not abandon them for a moment. Its premises are men, not in any fantastic isolation and rigidity, but in their actual, empirically perceptible process of development under definite conditions. As soon as this active life-process is described, history ceases to be a collection of dead facts as it is with the empiricists (themselves still abstract), or an imagined activity of imagined subjects, as with the idealists.[14]

---

14 On this statement, Marxism is thus both a form of realism, and a form of humanism. This leaves two accusations — or, I suppose, *interpretations* — regularly levelled at Marx's writings looking like nonsense. The first is the idea that Marxism is a sort of rigid "ideology" (often in contrast to the more practical, empirical capitalism — which "really works" in the "real world"). This cannot possibly be true: in accordance with Marx's method, any rigidly prescriptive teleology must be abandoned — and indeed, one of the most powerful and enduring aspects of Marx's account is the way in which he helps us understand capitalism's own dogmas as the ideology of those who happen to be in power. See also n. 27 below. The second is the idea, popularised by the likes of Althusser (some people think it should be illegal not to mention that Althusser murdered his wife whenever you invoke him, so here's me paying lip service to that) — the *wife murderer* Louis Althusser — that Marx should be understood as a sort of "anti-humanist". This interpretation is fine, perhaps, so long as

Where speculation ends — in real life — there real, positive science begins: the representation of the practical activity, of the practical process of development of men. Empty talk about consciousness ceases, and real knowledge has to take its place. When reality is depicted, philosophy as an independent branch of knowledge loses its medium of existence. At the best its place can only be taken by a summing-up of the most general results, abstractions which arise from the observation of the historical development of men. Viewed apart from real history, these abstractions have in themselves no value whatsoever. They can only serve to facilitate the arrangement of historical material, to indicate the sequence of its separate strata. But they by no means afford a recipe or schema, as does philosophy, for neatly trimming the epochs of history.[15] On the contrary, our difficulties begin only when we set about the observation and the arrangement — the real depiction-of our historical material, whether of a past epoch or of the present. The removal of these difficulties is governed by premises which it is quite impossible to state here, but which only the study of the actual life-process and the activity of the individuals of each epoch will make

---

you suppose that to be "human" must be to embody a set of fixed traits, defined top-down. But this is not the case, for Marx, at all. Marx places humanity at the bottom of all things: his theory of history, here in *The German Ideology*, and in his theory of how capitalism works, with the idea of "surplus-value" in *Capital vol. 1*. (*Capital*, in many ways, is a vast elaboration on Oedipus's answer to the riddle of the Sphinx: "that being is man"). Marx is a humanist for whom "humanity" does *not* consist in a series of rigidly fixed traits, but rather exists in a transformative, that is historical, relationship with the world. See also n. 41 below.

15 Again, we see how Marx is taking a realist view of history here. These lines ought rightly to surprise anyone who thinks that Marx has a rigidly teleological philosophy of history.

evident. We shall select here some of these abstractions, which we use in contradistinction to the ideologists, and shall illustrate them by historical examples.

History: Fundamental Conditions

Since we are dealing with the Germans, who are devoid of premises,[16] we must begin by stating the first premise of all human existence and, therefore, of all history, the premise, namely, that men must be in a position to live in order to be able to "make history". But life involves before everything else eating and drinking, a habitation,

---

16 Hegelian philosophy is supposed to be radically presuppositionless: his *Science of Logic*, in particular, attempts to reconstruct all of the categories of experience from the thinking of "being, pure being." We can think of this as a sort of radicalisation of Descartes. Descartes wanted to put science on a sure footing, by eliminating any illegitimate presuppositions (the legacy, for instance, of mere habit). He did this, in the *Meditations*, by assuming a sceptical attitude to everything, then reconstructing knowledge from the one thing that cannot be doubted. Even in his doubting of everything, he is still thinking — "I think, therefore I am." Ultimately, however, Descartes's project is miscarried in at least two ways. Most famously, he is only able to assure himself of the reality of the external world by putting into his head the 'innate idea' of an all-powerful, all-loving God, who would not trick him by making the whole thing illusory. But also: he has no reason to infer the existence of the self from the fact that he cannot doubt, in his doubt, that thinking is going on. In doubting everything, all Descartes know is that *the activity of thinking* is going on: "there is thinking, therefore...?" Hegel takes his starting point from thinking as such, and builds up the world (without any sort of load-bearing God) from there.

clothing and many other things. The first historical act is thus the production of the means to satisfy these needs, the production of material life itself. And indeed this is an historical act, a fundamental condition of all history, which today, as thousands of years ago, must daily and hourly be fulfilled merely in order to sustain human life. Even when the sensuous world is reduced to a minimum, to a stick as with Saint Bruno,[17] it presupposes the action of producing the stick. Therefore in any interpretation of history one has first of all to observe this fundamental fact in all its significance and all its implications and to accord it its due importance. It is well known that the Germans have never done this, and they have never, therefore, had an *earthly* basis for history and consequently never an historian. The French and the English, even if they have conceived

---

17 That is, Bruno Bauer. Bauer was a prominent member of the Young Hegelians, and was of course the second of the three figures Marx and Engels were concerned to critique in *The German Ideology* — although I've not included any of the Bauer section here. Marx had already conducted extensive critiques of Bauer in "On the Jewish Question" and *The Holy Family* (the titular "Family" being the Bauers — Bruno and his brother Edgar, a man so committed to idealism that he once tried to argue in court that he shouldn't be convicted of a crime because he didn't believe the state had any actual existence; he later worked as a spy in London for the Danish state, tasked with reporting, among others, on Marx — who he once lost his temper with and punched in the face). Probably the best Bauer-critique to read is "On the Jewish Question": the anti-Semitic Bruno thought that the political emancipation of the Jews required the abolition of the Jewish religion; Marx pushed Bruno's logic to its limits, and argued instead that political emancipation (for anyone, really) can only be achieved through the abolition of the (capitalist) state.

the relation of this fact with so-called history only in an extremely one-sided fashion, particularly as long as they remained in the toils of political ideology, have nevertheless made the first attempts to give the writing of history a materialistic basis by being the first to write histories of civil society, of commerce and industry.

The second point is that the satisfaction of the first need (the action of satisfying, and the instrument of satisfaction which has been acquired) leads to new needs; and this production of new needs is the first historical act.[18] Here we recognise immediately the spiritual ancestry of the great historical wisdom of the Germans who, when they run out of positive material and when they can serve up neither theological nor political nor literary rubbish, assert that this is not history at all, but the "prehistoric era". They do not, however, enlighten us as to how we proceed from this nonsensical "prehistory" to history proper; although, on the other hand, in their historical speculation they seize upon this "prehistory" with especial eagerness because they imagine themselves safe there from interference on the part of "crude facts", and, at the same time, because there they can give full rein to their speculative impulse and set up and knock down hypotheses by the thousand.

The third circumstance which, from the very outset, enters into historical development, is that men, who daily remake their own life, begin to make other men, to propagate their kind: the relation between man and woman, parents and children, the *family*. The family, which to begin with is the only social relationship, becomes later, when increased needs create new social relations and the

---

18 Here we have Marx and Engels's definition of humanity. Man is a "historical animal": an animal which, unique among the creation, is unable to obtain the things it needs in order to survive without inadvertently producing the need for something else.

increased population new needs, a subordinate one (except in Germany), and must then be treated and analysed according to the existing empirical data, not according to "the concept of the family", as is the custom in Germany.[19] These three aspects of social activity are not of course to be taken as three different stages, but just as three aspects or, to make it clear to the Germans, three "moments", which have existed simultaneously since the dawn of history and the first men, and which still assert themselves in history today.

---

19 *Marx and Engels include a footnote here, which will be grist to the mill of any contemporary "family abolitionists"*: "The building of houses. With savages each family has as a matter of course its own cave or hut like the separate family tent of the nomads. This separate domestic economy is made only the more necessary by the further development of private property. With the agricultural peoples a communal domestic economy is just as impossible as a communal cultivation of the soil. A great advance was the building of towns. In all previous periods, however, the abolition of individual economy, which is inseparable from the abolition of private property, was impossible for the simple reason that the material conditions governing it were not present. The setting-up of a communal domestic economy presupposes the development of machinery, of the use of natural forces and of many other productive forces — e.g. of water-supplies, of gas-lighting, steam-heating, etc., the removal of the antagonism of town and country. Without these conditions a communal economy would not in itself form a new productive force; lacking any material basis and resting on a purely theoretical foundation, it would be a mere freak and would end in nothing more than a monastic economy. What was possible can be seen in the towns brought about by condensation and the erection of communal buildings for various definite purposes (prisons, barracks, etc.). That the abolition of individual economy is inseparable from the abolition of the family is self-evident."

The production of life, both of one's own in labour and of fresh life in procreation, now appears as a double relationship: on the one hand as a natural, on the other as a social relationship. By social we understand the co-operation of several individuals, no matter under what conditions, in what manner and to what end. It follows from this that a certain mode of production, or industrial stage, is always combined with a certain mode of co-operation, or social stage, and this mode of co-operation is itself a "productive force". Further, that the multitude of productive forces accessible to men determines the nature of society, hence, that the "history of humanity" must always be studied and treated in relation to the history of industry and exchange. But it is also clear how in Germany it is impossible to write this sort of history, because the Germans lack not only the necessary power of comprehension and the material but also the "evidence of their senses", for across the Rhine you cannot have any experience of these things since history has stopped happening.[20] Thus it is quite obvious from the start that there exists a materialistic conception of men with one another, which is determined by their needs and their mode of production, and which is as old as men themselves. This connection is ever taking on new forms, and thus presents a "history" independently of the

---

20 Thus for Marx and Engels, it is Germany's economic "backwardness" that has turned the Germans into "ideologists" (or: into idealists). Obviously, these ideas are then able to take on a life of their own: presented as eternal wisdom, in academic philosophy departments their authors can be taken at their word. And so — material conditions permitting — you can dedicate your life to endlessly attempting to iron out the unironable creases in Kantian ethics (to name just one example). See also the section on Stirner's critique of political liberalism later on.

existence of any political or religious nonsense which in addition may hold men together.

Only now, after having considered four moments, four aspects of the primary historical relationships, do we find that man also possesses "consciousness", but, even so, not inherent, not "pure" consciousness. From the start the "spirit" is afflicted with the curse of being "burdened" with matter, which here makes its appearance in the form of agitated layers of air, sounds, in short, of language. Language is as old as consciousness, language is practical consciousness that exists also for other men, and for that reason alone it really exists for me personally as well; language, like consciousness, only arises from the need, the necessity, of intercourse with other men. Where there exists a relationship, it exists for me: the animal does not enter into "*relations*" with anything, it does not enter into any relation at all. For the animal, its relation to others does not exist as a relation. Consciousness is, therefore, from the very beginning a social product, and remains so as long as men exist at all. Consciousness is at first, of course, merely consciousness concerning the *immediate* sensuous environment and consciousness of the limited connection with other persons and things outside the individual who is growing self-conscious. At the same time it is consciousness of nature, which first appears to men as a completely alien, all-powerful and unassailable force, with which men's relations are purely animal and by which they are overawed like beasts; it is thus a purely animal consciousness of nature (natural religion) just because nature is as yet hardly modified historically. (We see here immediately: this natural religion or this particular relation of men to nature is determined by the form of society and vice versa. Here, as everywhere, the identity of nature and man appears in such a way that the restricted relation of men to nature determines their restricted relation to one another, and their restricted relation to one another determines men's restricted relation to nature.) On the other hand, man's consciousness of the necessity of associating with the individuals around him is the beginning of the consciousness that he is living in society at all. This beginning is as animal as social life itself at this stage. It is mere herd consciousness, and at this point man is only distinguished from sheep by the fact that with him consciousness takes the place of instinct or that his instinct is a conscious one. This sheep-like or tribal consciousness receives its further development and extension through increased productivity, the increase of needs, and, what is fundamental to both of these, the increase of population. With these there develops the division of labour, which was originally nothing but the division of labour in the sexual act, then that division of labour which develops spontaneously or "naturally" by virtue of natural predisposition (e.g. physical strength), needs, accidents, etc. etc. Division of labour only becomes truly such from the moment when a division of material and mental labour appears. (The first form of ideologists, *priests*, is concurrent.) From this moment onwards consciousness *can* really flatter itself that it is something other than consciousness of existing practice, that it *really* represents something without representing something real; from now on consciousness is in a position to emancipate itself from the world and to proceed to the formation of "pure" theory, theology, philosophy, ethics, etc. But even if this theory, theology, philosophy, ethics, etc. comes into contradiction with the existing relations, this can only occur because existing social relations have come into contradiction with existing forces of production; this, moreover, can also occur in a particular national sphere of relations through the appearance of the contradiction, not within the national orbit, but between this national consciousness and the practice of other nations, i.e. between the national and the general consciousness of a nation (as we see it now in Germany).

Moreover, it is quite immaterial what consciousness starts to do on its own: out of all such muck we get only the one inference that these three moments, the forces of production, the state of society, and consciousness, can and must come into contradiction with one another, because the division of labour implies the possibility, nay the fact that intellectual and material activity — enjoyment and labour, production and consumption — devolve on different individuals, and that the only possibility of their not coming into contradiction lies in the negation in its turn of the *division* of labour. It is self-evident, moreover, that "spectres", "bonds", "the higher being", "concept", "scruple", are merely the idealistic, spiritual expression, the conception apparently of the isolated individual, the image of very empirical fetters and limitations, within which the mode of production of life and the form of intercourse coupled with it move.

Private Property and Communism

With the division of labour, in which all these contradictions are implicit, and which in its turn is based on the natural division of labour in the family and the separation of society into individual families opposed to one another, is given simultaneously the *distribution*, and indeed the *unequal* distribution, both quantitative and qualitative, of labour and its products, hence property: the nucleus, the first form of which, lies in the family, where wife and children are the slaves of the husband. This latent slavery in the family, though still very crude, is the first property, but even at this early stage it corresponds perfectly to the definition of modern economists who call it the power of disposing of the labour-power of others. Division of labour and private property arc, moreover, identical expressions: in the one the same thing is affirmed with reference to activity as is affirmed in the other with reference to the product of the activity.

Further, the division of labour implies the contradiction between the interest of the separate individual or the individual family and the communal interest of all individuals who have intercourse with one another. And indeed, this communal interest does not exist merely in the imagination, as the "general interest", but first of all in reality, as the mutual interdependence of the individuals among whom the labour is divided.

And out of this very contradiction between the interest of the individual and that of the community the latter takes an independent form as the *State*, divorced from the real interests of individual and community, and at the same time as an illusory communal life, always based, however, on the real ties existing in every family and tribal conglomeration — such as flesh and blood, language, division of labour on a larger scale, and other interests — and especially, as we shall enlarge upon later, on the classes, already determined by the division of labour, which in every such mass of men separate out, and of which one dominates all the others. It follows from this that all struggles within the State, the struggle between democracy, aristocracy, and monarchy, the struggle for the franchise, etc., are merely the illusory forms in which the real struggles of the different classes are fought out among one another (of this the German theoreticians have not the faintest inkling, although they have received a sufficient introduction to the subject in the *Deutsch-Französische Jahrbucher* and *The Holy Family*).[21] Further, it follows that

---

21 Marx and Engels often refer in these manuscripts to the *Deutsch-Französische Jahrbucher,* which was a journal Marx published

every class which is struggling for mastery, even when its domination, as is the case with the proletariat, postulates the abolition of the old form of society in its entirety and of domination itself, must first conquer for itself political power in order to represent its interest in turn as the general interest, which in the first moment it is forced to do. Just because individuals seek *only* their particular interest, which for them does not coincide with their communal interest (in fact the general is the illusory form of communal life), the latter will be imposed on them as an interest "alien" to them, and "independent" of them as in its turn a particular, peculiar "general" interest; or they themselves must remain within this discord, as in democracy. On the other hand, too, the *practical* struggle of these particular interests, which constantly really run counter to the communal and illusory communal interests, makes *practical* intervention and control necessary through the illusory "general" interest in the form of the State.[22]

And finally, the division of labour offers us the first example of how, as long as man remains in natural society, that is, as long as a cleavage exists between the particular and the common interest, as long, therefore, as activity is not voluntarily, but naturally, divided, man's own deed becomes an alien power opposed to him, which enslaves

---

in Paris in collaboration with Arnold Ruge. It ran for only one edition, which contained "On the Jewish Question" (see n. 17 above), as well as "Introduction to a Critique of Hegel's *Philosophy of Right*", which is the essay where Marx makes his famous(ly misunderstood) crack about religion being the "opium of the masses." For *The Holy Family*, see n. 17 above.

22 Here we see a version of the point that we will find prominently underscored in the chapter on Stirner: for Marx and Engels, if "class consciousness" is to mean anything at all, then egoism and class consciousness must coincide.

him instead of being controlled by him. For as soon as the distribution of labour comes into being, each man has a particular, exclusive sphere of activity, which is forced upon him and from which he cannot escape. He is a hunter, a fisherman, a herdsman, or a critical critic, and must remain so if he does not want to lose his means of livelihood; while in communist society, where nobody has one exclusive sphere of activity but each can become accomplished in any branch he wishes, society regulates the general production and thus makes it possible for me to do one thing today and another tomorrow, to hunt in the morning, fish in the afternoon, rear cattle in the evening, criticise after dinner, just as I have a mind, without ever becoming hunter, fisherman, herdsman or critic.

This fixation of social activity, this consolidation of what we ourselves produce into an objective power above us, growing out of our control, thwarting our expectations, bringing to naught our calculations, is one of the chief factors in historical development up till now. The social power, i.e. the multiplied productive force, which arises through the co-operation of different individuals as it is determined by the division of labour, appears to these individuals, since their co-operation is not voluntary but has come about naturally, not as their own muted power, but as an alien force existing outside them, of the origin and goal of which they are ignorant, which they thus cannot control, which on the contrary passes through a peculiar series of phases and stages independent of the will and the action of man, nay even being the prime governor of these.

How otherwise could, for instance, property have had a history at all, have taken on different forms, and landed property, for example, according to the different premises given, have proceeded in France from parcellation to centralisation in the hands of a few, in England from centralisation in the hands of a few to parcellation, as is actually the case today? Or how does it happen that trade, which after all is nothing more than the exchange of products of various individuals and countries, rules the whole world through the relation of supply and demand — a relation which, as an English economist says, hovers over the earth like the fate of the ancients, and with invisible hand allots fortune and misfortune to men, sets up empires and overthrows empires, causes nations to rise and to disappear[23] — while with the abolition of the basis of private property, with the communistic regulation of production (and, implicit in this, the destruction of the alien relation between men and what they themselves produce), the power of the relation of supply and demand is dissolved into nothing, and men get exchange, production, the mode of their mutual relation, under their own control again?

In history up to the present it is certainly an empirical fact that separate individuals have, with the broadening of their activity into world-historical activity, become more and more enslaved under a power alien to them (a pressure which they have conceived of as a dirty trick on the part of the so-called universal spirit, etc.), a power which has become more and more enormous and, in the last instance, turns out to be the *world market*. But it is just as empirically established that, by the overthrow of the existing state of society by the communist revolution (of which more below) and the abolition of private property which is identical with it, this power, which so baffles the German theoreticians, will be dissolved; and that then the liberation of each single individual will be accomplished in the measure in which history becomes

---

23 Obviously it would be remiss of me not to point out that Marx and Engels are talking about Adam Smith here, who was not English but Scottish. Perhaps, like some early modern Andy Murray, he was English when writing the *Wealth of Nations*, but Scottish when he did the *Theory of Moral Sentiments*.

transformed into world history. From the above it is clear that the real intellectual wealth of the individual depends entirely on the wealth of his real connections. Only then will the separate individuals be liberated from the various national and local barriers, be brought into practical connection with the material and intellectual production of the whole world and be put in a position to acquire the capacity to enjoy this all-sided production of the whole earth (the creations of man). *All-round* dependence, this natural form of the *world-historical* co-operation of individuals, will be transformed by this communist revolution into the control and conscious mastery[24] of these powers, which, born of the action of men on one another, have till now overawed and governed men as powers completely alien to them. Now this view can be expressed again in speculative-idealistic, i.e. fantastic, terms as "self-generation of the species" ("society as the subject"), and thereby the consecutive series of interrelated individuals

---

24 Smith opens the *Wealth of Nations* by giving us the very typically eighteenth-century image of some primitive "hunters and fishers" who live on some island paradise and have everything in abundance. *Prima facie*, our own existence contrasts very unfavourably with theirs — so why has "historical progress", such as it is, favoured us, rather than them? The answer Smith gives is that his (imagined) savages are perennially subject to disasters beyond their control — they have no conscious mastery, in short, of the things they need in order to survive. Here, Marx and Engels remain very much within this Smithian riddle of history. With the advent of industrialism, more and more of the world has come within the conscious scope of human control — but that has been experienced as a *loss* of power by the worker. Communism will (Marx and Engels suppose) correct this, by placing everything within what we might best understand as a sort of "democratic" (though not, of course, liberal-democratic, electoral) control.

connected with each other can be conceived as a single individual, which accomplishes the mystery of generating itself. It is clear here that individuals certainly make *one another*, physically and mentally, but do not make themselves.

This "alienation" (to use a term which will be comprehensible to the philosophers)[25] can, of course, only be abolished given two *practical* premises. For it to become an "intolerable" power, i.e. a power against which men make a revolution, it must necessarily have rendered the great mass of humanity "propertyless", and produced, at the same time, the contradiction of an existing world of wealth and culture, both of which conditions presuppose a great increase in productive power, a high degree of its development. And, on the other hand, this development of productive forces (which itself implies the actual empirical existence of men in their *world-historical*, instead of local, being) is an absolutely necessary practical premise because without it *want* is merely made general, and with *destitution* the struggle for necessities and all the old filthy business would necessarily be reproduced; and furthermore, because only with this universal development of productive forces is a *universal* intercourse between men established, which produces in all nations simultaneously the phenomenon of the "propertyless" mass (universal competition), makes each nation dependent on the revolutions of the

---

25 Marx here seems to ridicule the term "alienation" (*Entfremdung*), which is a centrally important concept in Feuerbach — but of course he had himself written (see n. 10) a piece on "Alienated Labour" a couple of years previously (that said, he had no plans to publish it — and indeed, much like *The German Ideology* itself, it would not be published in Marx's lifetime). Essentially, if you are "alienated" from something, you lack what Marx and Engels above call "conscious mastery" of it (for Feuerbach, God is the alienated essence of Man).

others, and finally has put *world-historical*, empirically universal individuals in place of local ones.[26] Without this, (1) communism could only exist as a local event; (2) the *forces* of intercourse themselves could not have developed as *universal*, hence intolerable powers: they would have remained home-bred conditions surrounded by superstition; and (3) each extension of intercourse would abolish local communism. Empirically, communism is only possible as the act of the dominant peoples 'all at once' and simultaneously, which presupposes the universal development of productive forces and the world intercourse bound up with communism. Moreover, the mass of *propertyless* workers — the utterly precarious position of labour-power on a mass scale cut off from capital or from even a limited satisfaction and, therefore, no longer merely temporarily deprived of work itself as a secure source of life — presupposes the *world market* through competition. The proletariat can thus only exist *world-historically*, just as communism, its activity, can only have a 'world-historical' existence. World-historical existence of individuals means existence of individuals which is directly linked up with world history.

Communism is for us not a *state of affairs* which is to be established, an ideal to which reality will have to adjust itself. We call communism the *real* movement which abolishes the present state of things. The conditions of this movement result from the premises now in existence.[27]

---

26 This process is exactly the one that Marx and Engels would later describe in the first part of *The Communist Manifesto*.

27 This insight is, in my view, perhaps the single most important thing to take away from this text: if you're going to pay attention to any of it, in any way at all, then *this* is the thing to make sure you've absorbed. "Communism", for Marx and Engels, cannot be some fixed ideal, the sort of thing that might be nice in

B. The Illusion of the Epoch

Civil Society and the Conception of History

The form of intercourse determined by the existing productive forces at all previous historical stages, and in its turn determining these, is *civil society*.[28] The latter, as is clear from what we have said above, has as its premises and basis the simple family and the multiple, the so-called tribe, the more precise determinants of this society are enumerated in our remarks above. Already here we see how this civil society is the true source and theatre of all history, and how absurd is the conception of history held hitherto, which neglects the real relationships and confines itself to high-sounding dramas of princes and states.

Civil society embraces the whole material intercourse of individuals within a definite stage of the development of productive forces. It embraces the whole commercial and industrial life of a given stage and, insofar, transcends the State and the nation, though, on the other hand again, it must assert itself in its foreign relations as nationality, and inwardly must organise itself as State. The word

---

theory, but can never work in practice. It is, rather, the name of a movement, which proceeds (in an emancipatory fashion) from *how things are right now*. This, incidentally, is itself a reason to refuse to remain dogmatically wedded to anything Marx and Engels might happen to argue — "Communism" is a possibility we must look for *now*, in our *own* present; of course Marx's writings can be very helpful in articulating it, but that is no reason to treat them, theologically, as prophecies.

28 In German the phrase is *bürgerliche Gesellschaft*: literally, "bourgeois society". It is also the title of one of the most important sections of Hegel's *Philosophy of Right*.

"civil society" emerged in the eighteenth century, when property relationships had already extricated themselves from the ancient and medieval communal society. Civil society as such only develops with the bourgeoisie; the social organisation evolving directly out of production and commerce, which in all ages forms the basis of the State and of the rest of the idealistic superstructure, has, however, always been designated by the same name.

History is nothing but the succession of the separate generations, each of which exploits the materials, the capital funds, the productive forces handed down to it by all preceding generations, and thus, on the one hand, continues the traditional activity in completely changed circumstances and, on the other, modifies the old circumstances with a completely changed activity. This can be speculatively distorted so that later history is made the goal of earlier history, e.g. the goal ascribed to the discovery of America is to further the eruption of the French Revolution. Thereby history receives its own special aims and becomes "a person ranking with other persons" (to wit: "Self-Consciousness, Criticism, the Unique", etc.), while what is designated with the words "destiny", "goal", "germ", or "idea" of earlier history is nothing more than an abstraction formed from later history, from the active influence which earlier history exercises on later history.

The further the separate spheres, which interact on one another, extend in the course of this development, the more the original isolation of the separate nationalities is destroyed by the developed mode of production and intercourse and the division of labour between various nations naturally brought forth by these, the more history becomes world history. Thus, for instance, if in England a machine is invented, which deprives countless workers of bread in India and China, and overturns the whole form of existence of these empires, this invention becomes a world-historical fact. Or again, take the case of sugar and coffee which have proved their world-historical importance in the nineteenth century by the fact that the lack of these products, occasioned by the Napoleonic Continental System, caused the Germans to rise against Napoleon, and thus became the real basis of the glorious Wars of Liberation of 1813. From this it follows that this transformation of history into world history is not indeed a mere abstract act on the part of the "self-consciousness", the world spirit, or of any other metaphysical spectre, but a quite material, empirically verifiable act, an act the proof of which every individual furnishes as he comes and goes, eats, drinks and clothes himself.

This conception of history depends on our ability to expound the real process of production, starting out from the material production of life itself, and to comprehend the form of intercourse connected with this and created by this mode of production (i.e. civil society in its various stages), as the basis of all history; and to show it in its action as State, to explain all the different theoretical products and forms of consciousness, religion, philosophy, ethics, etc. and trace their origins and growth from that basis; by which means, of course, the whole thing can be depicted in its totality (and therefore, too, the reciprocal action of these various sides on one another). It has not, like the idealistic view of history, in every period to look for a category, but remains constantly on the real *ground* of history; it does not explain practice from the idea but explains the formation of ideas from material practice; and accordingly it comes to the conclusion that all forms and products of consciousness cannot be dissolved by mental criticism, by resolution into "self-consciousness" or transformation into "apparitions", "spectres", "fancies", etc. but only by the practical overthrow of the actual social relations which gave rise to this idealistic humbug[29]; that not criticism but revolution is the driving force of history, also of religion, of philosophy and all other types of theory. It shows that history does not end by being resolved into "self-consciousness" as "spirit of the spirit", but that in it at each stage there is found a material result: a sum of productive forces, an historically created relation of individuals to nature and to one another, which is handed down to each generation from its predecessor; a mass of productive forces, capital funds and conditions, which, on the one hand, is indeed modified by the new generation, but also on the other prescribes for it its conditions of life and gives it a definite development, a special character. It shows that circumstances make men just as much as men make circumstances.

This sum of productive forces, capital funds and social forms of intercourse, which every individual and generation finds in existence as something given, is the real basis of what the philosophers have conceived as "substance" and "essence of man", and what they have deified and attacked; a real basis which is not in the least disturbed, in its effect and influence on the development of men, by the fact that these philosophers revolt against it as "self-consciousness" and the "Unique". These conditions of life, which different generations find in existence, decide also whether or not the periodically recurring revolutionary convulsion will be strong enough to overthrow the basis of the entire existing system. And if these material elements of a complete

---

29 It can thus be seen that in their anti-idealism, Marx and Engels in fact take "ideas", as such, much more seriously than their Young Hegelian counterparts. Only from their materialistic perspective are we given some sense of why (bad) ideas might stick around.

revolution are not present (namely, on the one hand the existing productive forces, on the other the formation of a revolutionary mass, which revolts not only against separate conditions of society up till then, but against the very "production of life" till then, the "total activity" on which it was based), then, as far as practical development is concerned, it is absolutely immaterial whether the *idea* of this revolution has been expressed a hundred times already, as the history of communism proves.

In the whole conception of history up to the present this real basis of history has either been totally neglected or else considered as a minor matter quite irrelevant to the course of history. History must, therefore, always be written according to an extraneous standard; the real production of life seems to be primeval history, while the truly historical appears to be separated from ordinary life, something extra-superterrestrial. With this the relation of man to nature is excluded from history and hence the antithesis of nature and history is created.[30] The exponents of this conception of history have consequently only been

---

30 As it happens, my PhD research was largely focused on an early Adorno essay entitled "The Idea of Natural-History", which argues — essentially — that neither "nature" nor "history" can be understood without the other: historical change is driven by natural causes, which are themselves in turn transformed by historical change. At the end of that essay, Adorno declares that "I submit myself, so to speak, to the authority of the materialist dialectic," claiming that "what has been said here" is in fact "only an interpretation of certain fundamental elements of the materialist dialect" — in short, aligning his analysis (which I would argue — indeed, have argued, in a paper entitled "Understanding Adorno on 'Natural-History'" — is essentially Wittgensteinian-therapeutic in form) with Marxism. Obviously there are also resonances here with what I wrote about *The German Ideology* and "philosophical therapy" in the Introduction.

able to see in history the political actions of princes and States, religious and all sorts of theoretical struggles, and in particular in each historical epoch have had to *share the illusion of that epoch*. For instance, if an epoch imagines itself to be actuated by purely "political" or "religious" motives, although "religion" and "politics" are only forms of its true motives, the historian accepts this opinion. The "idea", the "conception" of the people in question about their real practice, is transformed into the sole determining, active force, which controls and determines their practice. When the crude form in which the division of labour appears with the Indians and Egyptians calls forth the caste-system in their State and religion, the historian believes that the caste-system is the power which has produced this crude social form. While the French and the English at least hold by the political illusion, which is moderately close to reality, the Germans move in the realm of the "pure spirit", and make religious illusion the driving force of history. The Hegelian philosophy of history is the last consequence, reduced to its "finest expression", of all this German historiography, for which it is not a question of real, nor even of political, interests, but of pure thoughts, which consequently must appear to Saint Bruno as a series of "thoughts" that devour one another and are finally swallowed up in "self-consciousness".

Ruling Class and Ruling Ideas

The ideas of the ruling class are in every epoch the ruling ideas, i.e. the class which is the ruling *material* force of society, is at the same time its ruling *intellectual* force. The class which has the means of material production at its disposal, has control at the same time over the means of mental production, so that thereby, generally speaking, the ideas of those who lack the means of mental production are subject to it. The ruling ideas are nothing more than the ideal expression of the dominant material relationships, the dominant material relationships grasped as ideas; hence of the relationships which make the one class the ruling one, therefore, the ideas of its dominance. The individuals composing the ruling class possess among other things consciousness, and therefore think. Insofar, therefore, as they rule as a class and determine the extent and compass of an epoch, it is self-evident that they do this in its whole range, hence among other things rule also as thinkers, as producers of ideas, and regulate the production and distribution of the ideas of their age: thus their ideas are the ruling ideas of the epoch. For instance, in an age and in a country where royal power, aristocracy, and bourgeoisie are contending for mastery and where, therefore, mastery is shared, the doctrine of this separation of powers proves to be the dominant idea and is expressed as an "eternal law".

The division of labour, which we already saw above as one of the chief forces of history up till now, manifests itself also in the ruling class as the division of mental and material labour, so that inside this class one part appears as the thinkers of the class (its active, conceptive ideologists, who make the perfecting of the illusion of the class about itself their chief source of livelihood), while the others' attitude to these ideas and illusions is more passive and receptive, because they are in reality the active members of this class and have less time to make up illusions and ideas about themselves. Within this class this cleavage can even develop into a certain opposition and hostility between the two parts, which, however, in the case of a practical collision, in which the class itself is endangered, automatically comes to nothing, in which case there also vanishes the semblance that the ruling ideas were not the ideas of the ruling class and had a power distinct from the power of this class. The existence of revolutionary ideas in a particular period presupposes the existence of a revolutionary class; about the premises for the latter sufficient has already been said above.

If now in considering the course of history we detach the ideas of the ruling class from the ruling class itself and attribute to them an independent existence, if we confine ourselves to saying that these or those ideas were dominant at a given time, without bothering ourselves about the conditions of production and the producers of these ideas, if we thus ignore the individuals and world conditions which are the source of the ideas, we can say, for instance, that during the time that the aristocracy was dominant, the concepts honour, loyalty, etc. were dominant, during the dominance of the bourgeoisie the concepts freedom, equality, etc.[31] The ruling class itself on the whole imagines this to be so. This conception of history, which is common to all historians, particularly since the eighteenth century, will necessarily come up against the phenomenon that increasingly abstract ideas hold sway, i.e. ideas which increasingly take on the form of universality. For each new class which puts itself in the place of one ruling before it, is compelled, merely in order to carry through its aim, to represent its interest as the common interest of all the members of society, that is, expressed in ideal form: it has to give its ideas the form of universality, and represent them as the only rational, universally valid ones. The class making a revolution appears from the very start, if only

---

31 I suppose it's interesting in light of this to consider that nowadays, for some reason, the powers-that-be — in England, at least — have decided that the most praiseworthy quality in someone is to be "anti-woke"; to refuse to "virtue signal" by bowing down to the "orthodoxy" the ruling class have decided has been imposed upon them by the powerless.

because it is opposed to a class, not as a class but as the representative of the whole of society; it appears as the whole mass of society confronting the one ruling class. It can do this because, to start with, its interest really is more connected with the common interest of all other non-ruling classes, because under the pressure of hitherto existing conditions its interest has not yet been able to develop as the particular interest of a particular class. Its victory, therefore, benefits also many individuals of the other classes which are not winning a dominant position, but only insofar as it now puts these individuals in a position to raise themselves into the ruling class. When the French bourgeoisie overthrew the power of the aristocracy, it thereby made it possible for many proletarians to raise themselves above the proletariat, but only insofar as they become bourgeois. Every new class, therefore, achieves its hegemony only on a broader basis than that of the class ruling previously, whereas the opposition of the non-ruling class against the new ruling class later develops all the more sharply and profoundly. Both these things determine the fact that the struggle to be waged against this new ruling class, in its turn, aims at a more decided and radical negation of the previous conditions of society than could all previous classes which sought to rule.

This whole semblance, that the rule of a certain class is only the rule of certain ideas, comes to a natural end, of course, as soon as class rule in general ceases to be the form in which society is organised, that is to say, as soon as it is no longer necessary to represent a particular interest as general or the "general interest" as ruling.

Once the ruling ideas have been separated from the ruling individuals and, above all, from the relationships which result from a given stage of the mode of production, and in this way the conclusion has been reached that history is always under the sway of ideas, it is very easy to abstract from these various ideas "*the* idea", "the notion", etc. as the dominant force in history, and thus to understand all these separate ideas and concepts as "forms of self-determination" on the part of *the* concept developing in history. It follows then naturally, too, that all the relationships of men can be derived from the concept of man, the man as conceived, the essence of man, Man. This has been done by the speculative philosophers. Hegel himself confesses at the end of his *Philosophy of History* that he "has considered the progress of the *concept* only" and has represented in history the "true theodicy". Now one can go back again to the producers of the "concept", to the theorists, ideologists and philosophers, and one comes then to the conclusion that the philosophers, the thinkers as such, have at all times been dominant in history: a conclusion, as we see, already expressed by Hegel. The whole trick of proving the hegemony of the spirit in history (hierarchy, Stimer calls it) is thus confined to the following three efforts.

(1) One must separate the ideas of those ruling for empirical reasons, under empirical conditions and as empirical individuals, from these actual rulers, and thus recognise the rule of ideas or illusions in history.

(2) One must bring an order into this rule of ideas, prove a mystical connection among the successive ruling ideas; which is managed by understanding them as "acts of self-determination on the part of the concept" (this is possible because by virtue of their empirical basis these ideas are really connected with one another and because, conceived as *mere* ideas, they become self-distinctions, distinctions made by thought).

(3) To remove the mystical appearance of this "self-determining concept" it is changed into a person — "Self-Consciousness" — or, to appear thoroughly materialistic, into a series of persons, who represent the "concept" in history, into the "thinkers", the "philosophers", the ideologists, who again are understood as the manufacturers of history, as the "council of guardians", as the rulers. Thus the whole body of materialistic elements has been removed from history and now full reign can be given to the speculative steed.

Whilst in ordinary life every shopkeeper is very well able to distinguish between what somebody professes to be and what he really is, our historians have not yet won even this trivial insight. They take every epoch at its word and believe that everything it says and imagines about itself is true.

This historical method which reigned in Germany, and especially the reason why, must be understood from its connection with the illusion of ideologists in general, e.g. the illusions of the jurist, politicians (of the practical statesmen among them, too), from the dogmatic dreamings and distortions of these fellows; this is explained perfectly easily from their practical position in life, their job, and the division of labour.

C. Proletarians and Communism

Individuals, Class, and Community

In the Middle Ages the citizens in each town were compelled to unite against the landed nobility to save their skins. The extension of trade, the establishment of communications, led the separate towns to get to know other towns, which had asserted the same interests in the struggle with the same antagonist. Out of the many local corporations of burghers there arose only gradually the burgher class. The conditions of life of the individual burghers became, on account of their contradiction to the existing relationships and of the mode of labour determined by these, conditions which were common to them all and independent of each individual. The burghers had created the conditions insofar as they had torn themselves free from feudal ties, and were created by them insofar as they were determined by their antagonism to the feudal system which they found in existence. When the individual towns began to enter into associations, these common conditions developed into class conditions. The same conditions, the same contradiction, the same interests necessarily called forth on the whole similar customs everywhere. The bourgeoisie itself, with its conditions, develops only gradually, splits according to the division of labour into various fractions and finally absorbs all propertied classes it finds in existence (while it develops the majority of the earlier propertyless and a part of the hitherto propertied classes into a new class, the proletariat) in the measure to which all property found in existence is transformed into industrial or commercial capital. The separate individuals form a class only insofar as they have to carry on a common battle against another class; otherwise they are on hostile terms with each other as competitors. On the other hand, the class in its turn achieves an independent existence over against the individuals, so that the latter find their conditions of existence predestined, and hence have their position in life and their personal development assigned to them by their class, become subsumed under it. This is the same phenomenon as the subjection of the separate individuals to the division of labour and can only be removed by the abolition of private property and of labour itself. We have already indicated several times how this subsuming of individuals under the class brings with it their subjection to all kinds of ideas, etc.

If from a *philosophical* point of view one considers this evolution of individuals in the common conditions of existence of estates and classes, which followed on one another, and in the accompanying general conceptions forced upon them, it is certainly very easy to imagine that in these individuals the species, or "Man", has evolved, or that they evolved "Man" — and in this way one can give history some hard clouts on the ear.[32] One can conceive these various estates and classes to be specific terms of the general expression, subordinate varieties of the species, or evolutionary phases of "Man".

This subsuming of individuals under definite classes cannot be abolished until a class has taken shape, which has no longer any particular class interest to assert against the ruling class.

The transformation, through the division of labour, of personal powers (relationships) into material powers, cannot be dispelled by dismissing the general idea of it from one's mind, but can only be abolished by the individuals again subjecting these material powers to themselves and abolishing the division of labour. This is not possible without the community. Only in community with others has each individual the means of cultivating his gifts in all directions; only in the community, therefore, is personal freedom possible. In the previous substitutes

---

32 *Footnote from Marx and Engels:* "The statement which frequently occurs with Saint Max that each is all that he is through the State is fundamentally the same as the statement that bourgeois is only a specimen of the bourgeois species; a statement which presupposes that the class of bourgeois existed before the individuals constituting it. With the philosophers, class is *pre-existent.*"

for the community, in the State, etc. personal freedom has existed only for the individuals who developed within the relationships of the ruling class, and only insofar as they were individuals of this class. The illusory community, in which individuals have up till now combined, always took on an independent existence in relation to them, and was at the same time, since it was the combination of one class over against another, not only a completely illusory community, but a new fetter as well. In a real community the individuals obtain their freedom in and through their association.[33]

Individuals have always built on themselves, but naturally on themselves within their given historical conditions and relationships, not on the "pure" individual in the sense of the ideologists. But in the course of historical evolution, and precisely through the inevitable fact that within the division of labour social relationships take on an independent existence, there appears a division within the life of each individual, insofar as it is personal and insofar as it is determined by some branch of labour and the conditions pertaining to it. (We do not mean it to be understood from this that, for example, the rentier, the capitalist, etc. cease to be persons; but their personality is conditioned and

---

33 These points will be elaborated on in greater detail in the Stirner chapter, as presented below. They relate to perhaps the key take-home message of the Stirner section, that is: if you were a really consistent egoist, if you really were pursuing your individual self-interest, then (provided you are a member of the proletariat, that is to say not a bourgeois) you would immediately be converted to Communism. The "rugged individualism" of American libertarians, which effectively preaches the freedom of corporations to do whatever they like with you, is the true gospel of idiot altruists — those who love nothing more than to toil in the service of another.

determined by quite definite class relationships, and the division appears only in their opposition to another class and, for themselves, only when they go bankrupt.) In the estate (and even more in the tribe) this is as yet concealed: for instance, a nobleman always remains a nobleman, a commoner always a commoner, apart from his other relationships, a quality inseparable from his individuality. The division between the personal and the class individual, the accidental nature of the conditions of life for the individual, appears only with the emergence of the class, which is itself a product of the bourgeoisie. This accidental character is only engendered and developed by competition and the struggle of individuals among themselves. Thus, in imagination, individuals seem freer under the dominance of the bourgeoisie than before, because their conditions of life seem accidental; in reality, of course, they are less free, because they are more subjected to the violence of things.[34] The difference from the estate comes out particularly in the antagonism between the bourgeoisie and the proletariat. When the estate of the urban burghers, the corporations, etc. emerged in opposition to the landed nobility, their condition of existence — movable property and craft labour, which had already existed latently before their separation from the feudal ties –appeared as something positive, which was asserted against feudal landed property, and, therefore, in its own way at first took on a feudal form. Certainly the refugee serfs treated their previous servitude

---

34 It is central to Marx's analysis of capitalism that under capitalism, labour is supposed to be "free" — the contrast here is with feudalism, in which labour is enserfed. The crucial point is that in capitalist society, workers are "free" to sell their labour (to the highest bidder) for a wage (as opposed to being tied to the land). The catch, of course, is that the alternative is to exercise your "freedom" to starve to death.

as something accidental to their personality. But here they only were doing what every class that is freeing itself from a fetter does; and they did not free themselves as a class but separately. Moreover, they did not rise above the system of estates, but only formed a new estate, retaining their previous mode of labour even in their new situation, and developing it further by freeing it from its earlier fetters, which no longer corresponded to the development already attained.[35]

For the proletarians, on the other hand: the condition of their existence — labour — and with it all the conditions of existence governing modern society, have become something accidental, something over which they, as separate individuals, have no control, and over which no social organisation can give them control. The contradiction between the individuality of each separate proletarian and labour, the condition of life forced upon him, becomes evident to him himself, for he is sacrificed from youth upwards and, within his own class, has no chance of arriving at the conditions which would place him in the other class.

Thus, while the refugee serfs only wished to be free to develop and assert those conditions of existence which were

---

35 *Footnote from Marx and Engels*: "It must not be forgotten that the serf's very need of existing and the impossibility of a large-scale economy, which involved the distribution of the allotments among the serfs, very soon reduced the services of the serfs to their lord to an average of payments in kind and statute-labour. This made it possible for the serf to accumulate movable property and hence facilitated his escape out of the possession of his lord and gave him the prospect of making his way as an urban citizen; it also created gradations among the serfs, so that the runaway serfs were already half burghers. It is likewise obvious that the serfs who were masters of a craft had the best chance of acquiring movable property."

already there, and hence, in the end, only arrived at free labour, the proletarians, if they are to assert themselves as individuals, will have to abolish the very condition of their existence hitherto (which has, moreover, been that of all society up to the present), namely, labour. Thus they find themselves directly opposed to the form in which, hitherto, the individuals, of which society consists, have given themselves collective expression, that is, the State. In order, therefore, to assert themselves as individuals, they must overthrow the State.[36]

It follows from all we have been saying up till now that the communal relationship into which the individuals of a class entered, and which was determined by their common interests over against a third party, was always a community to which these individuals belonged only as average individuals, only insofar as they lived within the conditions of existence of their class — a relationship in which they participated not as individuals but as members of a class. With the community of revolutionary proletarians, on the other hand, who take their conditions of existence and those of all members of society under their control, it is just the reverse; it is as individuals that the individuals participate in it. It is just this combination of individuals (assuming

---

36 See n. 33 above. The point here is really that: if we assume individuals are motivated by self-interest, then in a capitalist society the sum of individual self-interests will inevitably culminate in Communist revolution. The fact that this has not happened — at least, in the more developed West — is proof of either one or both of two things: (1) that Marx and Engels were mistaken in their class analysis — the very neat division they posit between bourgeois and proletariat, which renders the identification of one's self-interest idiot-proof; (2) people are not actually motivated primarily by self-interest — they are either more altruistic, or less rational than this (or both).

the advanced stage of modern productive forces, of course) which puts the conditions of the free development and movement of individuals under their control — conditions which were previously abandoned to chance and had won an independent existence over against the separate individuals just because of their separation as individuals, and because of the necessity of their combination which had been determined by the division of labour, and through their separation had become a bond alien to them. Combination up till now (by no means an arbitrary one, such as is expounded for example in Rousseau's *Social Contract*, but a necessary one) was an agreement upon these conditions, within which the individuals were free to enjoy the freaks of fortune (compare, e.g., the formation of the North American State and the South American republics). This right to the undisturbed enjoyment, within certain conditions, of fortuity and chance has up till now been called personal freedom. These conditions of existence are, of course, only the productive forces and forms of intercourse at any particular time.

Forms of Intercourse

Communism differs from all previous movements in that it overturns the basis of all earlier relations of production and intercourse, and for the first time consciously treats all natural premises as the creatures of hitherto existing men, strips them of their natural character and subjugates them to the power of the united individuals. Its organisation is, therefore, essentially economic, the material production of the conditions of this unity; it turns existing conditions into conditions of unity. The reality, which communism is creating, is precisely the true basis for rendering it impossible that anything should exist independently of individuals, insofar as reality is only a product of the preceding intercourse of individuals themselves. Thus the communists in practice treat the conditions created up to now by production and intercourse as inorganic conditions, without, however, imagining that it was the plan or the destiny of previous generations to give them material, and without believing that these conditions were inorganic for the individuals creating them.

The difference between the individual as a person and what is accidental to him, is not a conceptual difference but an historical fact. This distinction has a different significance at different times — e.g. the estate as something accidental to the individual in the eighteenth century, the family more or less too. It is not a distinction that we have to make for each age, but one which each age makes itself from among the different elements which it finds in existence, and indeed not according to any theory, but compelled by material collisions in life.

What appears accidental to the later age as opposed to the earlier — and this applies also to the elements handed down by an earlier age — is a form of intercourse which corresponded to a definite stage of development of the productive forces. The relation of the productive forces to the form of intercourse is the relation of the form of intercourse to the occupation or activity of the individuals. (The fundamental form of this activity is, of course, material, on which depend all other forms — mental, political, religious, etc. The various shaping of material life is, of course, in every case dependent on the needs which are already developed, and the production, as well as the satisfaction, of these needs is an historical process, which is not found in the case of a sheep or a dog, although sheep and dogs in their present form are certainly products of an historical process.) The conditions under which individuals have intercourse with each other, so long as the above-mentioned contradiction is absent, are conditions appertaining to their individuality, in no way external to them; conditions under which these definite individuals, living under definite relationships, can alone produce their material life and what is connected with it, are thus the conditions of their self-activity and are produced by this self-activity. The definite condition under which they produce, thus corresponds, as long as the contradiction has not yet appeared, to the reality of their conditioned nature, their one-sided existence, the one-sidedness of which only becomes evident when the contradiction enters on the scene and thus exists for the later individuals. Then this condition appears as an accidental fetter, and the consciousness that it is a fetter is imputed to the earlier age as well.

These various conditions, which appear first as conditions of self-activity, later as fetters upon it, form in the whole evolution of history a coherent series of forms of intercourse, the coherence of which consists in this: in the place of an earlier form of intercourse, which has become a fetter, a new one is put, corresponding to the more developed productive forces and, hence, to the advanced mode of the self-activity of individuals — a form which in its turn becomes a fetter and is then replaced by another. Since these conditions correspond at every stage to the simultaneous development of the productive forces, their history is at the same time the history of the evolving productive forces taken over by each new generation, and is, therefore, the history of the development of the forces of the individuals themselves.

Since this evolution takes place naturally, i.e. is not subordinated to a general plan of freely combined individuals, it proceeds from various localities, tribes, nations, branches of labour, etc. each of which to start with develops independently of the others and only gradually enters into relation with the others. Furthermore, it takes place only very slowly; the various stages and interests are never completely overcome, but only subordinated to the prevailing interest and trail along beside the latter for centuries afterwards. It follows from this that within a nation itself the individuals, even apart from their pecuniary circumstances, have quite different developments, and that an earlier interest, the peculiar form of intercourse of which has already been ousted by that belonging to a later interest, remains for a long time afterwards in possession of a traditional power in the illusory community (State, law), which has won an existence independent of the individuals; a power which in the last resort can only be broken by a revolution. This explains why, with reference to individual points which allow of a more general summing-up, consciousness can sometimes appear further advanced than the contemporary empirical relationships, so that in the struggles of a later epoch one can refer to earlier theoreticians as authorities.[37]

This contradiction between the productive forces and the form of intercourse, which, as we saw, has occurred several times in past history, without, however, endangering the basis, necessarily on each occasion burst out in a revolution, taking on at the same time various subsidiary forms, such as all-embracing collisions, collisions of various classes, contradiction of consciousness, battle of ideas, etc., political conflict, etc. From a narrow point of view one may isolate one of these subsidiary forms and consider it as the basis of these revolutions; and this is all the more easy as the individuals who started the revolutions had illusions about their own activity according to their degree of culture and the stage of historical development.

Thus all collisions in history have their origin, according to our view, in the contradiction between the productive forces and the form of intercourse. Incidentally, to lead

---

37 As, of course, we continue to refer to Marx (and Engels) today.

to collisions in a country, this contradiction need not necessarily have reached its extreme limit in this particular country. The competition with industrially more advanced countries, brought about by the expansion of international intercourse, is sufficient to produce a similar contradiction in countries with a backward industry. For instance, the latent proletariat in Germany have been brought into view by the competition of English industry.

Contradictions of Big Industry: Revolution

Our investigation hitherto started from the instruments of production, and it has already shown that private property was a necessity for certain industrial stages. In extractive industries private property still coincides with labour; in small industry and all agriculture up till now property is the necessary consequence of the existing instruments of production; in big industry[38] the contradiction between the instrument of production and private property appears from the first time and is the product of big industry; moreover, big industry must be highly developed to produce this contradiction. And thus only with big industry does the abolition of private property become possible.

In big industry and competition the whole mass of conditions of existence, limitations, biases of individuals, are fused together into the two simplest forms: private property and labour. With money every form of intercourse, and intercourse itself, is considered fortuitous for the individuals. Thus money implies that all previous intercourse was only intercourse of individuals under particular conditions, not of individuals as individuals. These conditions are reduced to two: accumulated labour or private property, and actual labour. If both or one of these ceases, then intercourse

---

38 So, you know: factories.

comes to a standstill. The modern economists themselves, e.g. Sismondi, Cherbuliez, etc., oppose "association of individuals" to "association of capital". On the other hand, the individuals themselves are entirely subordinated to the division of labour and hence are brought into the most complete dependence on one another. Private property, insofar as within labour itself it is opposed to labour, evolves out of the necessity of accumulation, and has still, to begin with, rather the form of the communality; but in its further development it approaches more and more the modern form of private property. The division of labour implies from the outset the division of the *conditions* of labour, of tools and materials, and thus the splitting-up of accumulated capital among different owners, and thus, also, the division between capital and labour, and the different forms of property itself. The more the division of labour develops and accumulation grows, the sharper are the forms that this process of differentiation assumes. Labour itself can only exist on the premise of this fragmentation.

Thus two facts are here revealed. First the productive forces appear as a world for themselves, quite independent of and divorced from the individuals, alongside the individuals: the reason for this is that the individuals, whose forces they are, exist split up and in opposition to one another, whilst, on the other hand, these forces are only real forces in the intercourse and association of these individuals. Thus, on the one hand, we have a totality of productive forces, which have, as it were, taken on a material form and are for the individuals no longer the forces of the individuals but of private property, and hence of the individuals only insofar as they are owners of private property themselves. Never, in any earlier period, have the productive forces taken on a form so indifferent to the intercourse of individuals as individuals, because their intercourse itself was formerly a restricted one. On the other hand, standing over against these productive forces, we have the majority of the individuals from whom these forces have been wrested away, and who, robbed thus of all real life-content, have become abstract individuals, but who are, however, only by this fact put into a position to enter into relation with one another *as individuals*.

The only connection which still links them with the productive forces and with their own existence — labour — has lost all semblance of self-activity and only sustains their life by stunting it.[39] While in the earlier periods self-activity and the production of material life were separated, in that they devolved on different persons, and while, on account of the narrowness of the individuals themselves, the production of material life was considered as a subordinate mode of self-activity, they now diverge to such an extent that altogether material life appears as the end, and what produces this material life, labour (which is now the only possible but, as we see, negative form of self-activity), as the means.

Thus things have now come to such a pass that the individuals must appropriate the existing totality of productive forces, not only to achieve self-activity, but, also, merely to safeguard their very existence. This appropriation is first determined by the object to be appropriated, the productive forces, which have been developed to a totality and which only exist within a universal intercourse. From this aspect alone, therefore, this appropriation must have a universal character corresponding to the productive forces and the intercourse.

---

39 This much is retained from the earlier chapter on "Alienated Labour" (see n. 10 above): the identification of labour with "self-activity", thus with the realisation of oneself both as an individual, and as a social being.

The appropriation of these forces is itself nothing more than the development of the individual capacities corresponding to the material instruments of production. The appropriation of a totality of instruments of production is, for this very reason, the development of a totality of capacities in the individuals themselves.

This appropriation is further determined by the persons appropriating. Only the proletarians of the present day, who are completely shut off from all self-activity, are in a position to achieve a complete and no longer restricted self-activity, which consists in the appropriation of a totality of productive forces and in the thus postulated development of a totality of capacities.[40] All earlier revolutionary appropriations were restricted; individuals, whose self-activity was restricted by a crude instrument of production and a limited intercourse, appropriated this crude instrument of production, and hence merely achieved a new state of limitation. Their instrument of production became their property, but they themselves remained subordinate to the division of labour and their own instrument of production. In all expropriation up to now, a mass of individuals remained subservient to a single instrument of production; in the appropriation by the proletarians, a mass of instruments of production must be made subject to each individual, and property to all. Modern universal intercourse can be controlled by individuals, therefore, only when controlled by all.

This appropriation is further determined by the manner in which it must be effected. It can only be effected through a union, which by the character of the proletariat itself can again only be a universal one, and through a revolution,

---

40 For more on this see the end of Marx's early text "On James Mill", where he talks about what it would be to "produce in a human way".

in which, on the one hand, the power of the earlier mode of production and intercourse and social organisation is overthrown, and, on the other hand, there develops the universal character and the energy of the proletariat, without which the revolution cannot be accomplished; and in which, further, the proletariat rids itself of everything that still clings to it from its previous position in society.[41]

Only at this stage does self-activity coincide with material life, which corresponds to the development of individuals into complete individuals and the casting-off of all natural

---

41 At this point in the dialectic, someone always twigs: well, of course, Marx and Engels are describing a class that has, as it were, *nothing to lose*. Nowadays, a revolution seems a long way off. But then maybe that's just because we've grown too comfortable on the spoils of what remains of the history of working class struggle: maybe what we *really* need is for everything to get even worse — for preference, as fast as it is possible for things to get worse (presumably, so they can get better again all the faster). This would be, in board outline, a sort of crude "accelerationism" (though any resemblance to actual "accelerationisms", past or present, that anyone has actually ever consistently argued for, may in truth be minimal – credit to Matt Colquhoun for pointing that out). Of course, aside from the various practical (not to mention moral) problems with this logic, just as a point of pure theory, it seems to miss what is for Marx and Engels most crucial about the position of the proletariat: the fact that, while in bourgeois society they are denied the spoils of their labour (or any autonomy over it), they are in fact *all-powerful* over the bourgeoisie, since the bourgeoisie completely rely on them in order to produce the things they need in order to survive. All the proletariat really need to do is definitively assume this theoretical position, and then realise it, and they will win. More misery means more weakness, means the revolution becomes less likely, not more.

limitations. The transformation of labour into self-activity corresponds to the transformation of the earlier limited intercourse into the intercourse of individuals as such. With the appropriation of the total productive forces through united individuals, private property comes to an end. Whilst previously in history a particular condition always appeared as accidental, now the isolation of individuals and the particular private gain of each man have themselves become accidental.

The individuals, who are no longer subject to the division of labour, have been conceived by the philosophers as an ideal, under the name "Man".[42] They have conceived the whole process which we have outlined as the evolutionary process of "Man", so that at every historical stage "Man" was substituted for the individuals and shown as the motive force of history. The whole process was thus conceived as a process of the self-estrangement of "Man", and this was essentially due to the fact that the average individual of the later stage was always foisted on to the earlier stage, and the consciousness of a later age on to the individuals of an earlier. Through this inversion, which from the first is an abstract image of the actual conditions, it was possible to transform the whole of history into an evolutionary process of consciousness.

Conclusion

Finally, from the conception of history we have sketched we obtain these further conclusions:

---

42 One way to contextualise this remark in relation to scholarly debates hinted at in n. 14 above: Marx is not an "anti-humanist". He is an anti-*Man*ist. He has set himself against *idealistic* understandings of "humanity", not the human species as a material reality.

(1) In the development of productive forces there comes a stage when productive forces and means of intercourse are brought into being, which, under the existing relationships, only cause mischief, and are no longer productive but destructive forces (machinery and money); and connected with this a class is called forth, which has to bear all the burdens of society without enjoying its advantages, which, ousted from society, is forced into the most decided antagonism to all other classes; a class which forms the majority of all members of society, and from which emanates the consciousness of the necessity of a fundamental revolution, the communist consciousness, which may, of course, arise among the other classes too through the contemplation of the situation of this class.

(2) The conditions under which definite productive forces can be applied are the conditions of the rule of a definite class of society, whose social power, deriving from its property, has its *practical*-idealistic expression in each case in the form of the State; and, therefore, every revolutionary struggle is directed against a class, which till then has been in power. (The people are interested in maintaining the present state of production).

(3) In all revolutions up till now the mode of activity always remained unscathed and it was only a question of a different distribution of this activity, a new distribution of labour to other persons, whilst the communist revolution is directed against the preceding *mode* of activity, does away with *labour*, and abolishes the rule of all classes with the classes themselves, because it is carried through by the class which no longer counts as a class in society, is not recognised as a class, and is in itself the expression of the dissolution of all classes, nationalities, etc. within present society.

(4) Both for the production on a mass scale of this communist consciousness, and for the success of the cause itself, the alteration of men on a mass scale is, necessary, an alteration which can only take place in a practical movement, a revolution; this revolution is necessary, therefore, not only because the ruling class cannot be overthrown in any other way, but also because the class overthrowing it can only in a revolution succeed because in ridding itself of all the muck of ages and become fitted to found society anew.

2. "III. SANKT MAX", OR: "THE CHAPTER ON STIRNER (HEAVILY ABRIDGED)", OR: "ON EGOISM AND CLASS CONSCIOUSNESS"

The Unique and His Property

The man who has "set his cause on nothing" begins his lengthy "critical hurrah" like a good German, straightaway with a jeremiad: "Is there anything that is not to be my cause?" And he continues lamenting heart-rendingly that "everything is to be his cause," that "God's cause, the cause of mankind, of truth and freedom, and in addition the cause of his people, of his lord," and thousands of other good causes, are imposed on him. The poor fellow!

The French and English bourgeois complain about lack of markets, trade crises, panic on the stock exchange, the political situation prevailing at the moment, etc.; the German petty bourgeois, whose active participation in the bourgeois movement has been merely an ideal one, and who for the rest exposed only himself to risk, sees his own cause simply as the "good cause", the "cause of freedom, truth, mankind", etc. Our German school-teacher[43] simply believes this illusion of the German petty bourgeois and on three pages he provisionally discusses all these good causes.

He investigates "God's cause," "the cause of mankind," and finds these are "purely egoistical causes," that both "God" and "mankind" worry only about what is *theirs*, that "truth, freedom, humanity, justice" are "only interested

---

43 Stirner worked as a teacher at a girl's school.

in themselves and not in us, only in their own well-being and not in ours" — from which he concludes that all these persons "are thereby exceptionally well-off." He goes so far as to transform these idealistic phrases — God, truth, etc. — into prosperous burghers who "are exceptionally well-off" and enjoy a *"profitable* egoism." But this vexes the holy egoist.

"And I?" he exclaims.

> "I, for my part, draw the lesson from this and, instead of continuing to serve these great egoists, I should rather be an egoist myself!"

Thus we see what holy motives guide Saint Max in his transition to egoism. It is not the good things of this world, not treasures which moth and rust corrupt, not the capital belonging to his fellow unique ones, but heavenly treasure, the capital which belongs to God, truth, freedom, mankind, etc., that gives him no peace. If it had not been expected of him that he should serve numerous good causes, he would never have made the discovery that he also has his "own" cause, and therefore he would never have based this cause of his "on nothing" (i.e. "the book").

If Saint Max had looked a little more closely at these various "causes" and the "owners" of these causes, e.g., God, mankind, truth, he would have arrived at the opposite conclusion: that egoism based on the egoistic mode of action of these persons must be just as imaginary as these persons themselves.[44]

---

44 In a letter to Marx dated 19/11/1844, Engels describes Stirner's book as follows: "This egoism is taken to such a pitch, it is so absurd and at the same time so self-aware, that it cannot maintain itself even for an instant in its one-sidedness, but must immediately change into communism."

Instead of this, our saint decides to enter into competition with "God" and "truth" and to base his cause on himself:

> "On myself, on the I that is, just as much as God, the nothing of everything else, the I that is everything for me, the I that is the unique… I am nothing in the sense of void, but the creative nothing, the nothing from which I myself, as creator, create everything."

The holy church father could also have expressed this last proposition as follows: I am everything in the void of nonsense, *but* I am the nugatory creator, the all, from which I myself, as creator, create nothing.

Which of these two readings is the correct one will become evident later. So much for the preface.

The "book" itself is divided like the book "of old", into the Old and New Testament: namely, into the unique history of man (the Law and the Prophets) and the inhuman history of the unique (the Gospel of the Kingdom of God).[45] The former is history in the framework of logic, the logos confined in the past; the latter is logic in history,

---

45 Stirner's book does not only imitate the Bible, but also Ludwig Feuerbach's *The Essence of Christianity*, which it is in many ways explicitly a critique of. Part 1 of Feuerbach's book is titled "The True or Anthropological Essence of Religion," Part 2 is titled "The False or Theological Essence of Religion." One way of reading *The German Ideology*: Marx and Engels never really needed to write a Feuerbach chapter (which is why they didn't) — Stirner had already carried out the relevant critique for them. Their critique of the Young Hegelian tradition takes it cues from where *he* left off. (Hence why the actual text of *The German Ideology* is so dominated by the chapter on Stirner.)

the emancipated logos, which struggles against the present and triumphantly overcomes it.

The Old Testament: Man

The Book of Genesis, i.e., A Man's Life

Saint Max pretends here that he is writing the *biography* of his mortal enemy, "*man*", and not of a "*unique*" or "real individual". This ties him up in some delightful contradictions.

As becomes every normal genesis, "a man's life" begins *ab ovo*,[46] with the "child". The child "from the outset lives a life of struggle against the entire world, it resists everything and everything resists it." "Both remain enemies" but "with awe and respect" and "are constantly on the watch, looking for each other's weaknesses." "We," as children, "try to find out the basis of things or what lies behind them; therefore" (so no longer out of enmity) "we are trying to discover everybody's weaknesses." Thus, the child immediately becomes a metaphysician, trying to find out the "basis of things."

This speculating child, for whom "the nature of things" lies closer to his heart than his toys, "sometimes" in the long run, succeeds in coping with the "world of things," conquers it and then enters a new phase, the age of youth, when he has to face a new "arduous struggle of life," the struggle against reason, for the "spirit means the first self-discovery" and: "We are above the world, we are spirit."

"The point of view of the youth is a 'heavenly one'; the child merely learned," "he did not dwell on purely logical or theological problems" — just as (the child) "Pilate"

---

46 "From the egg."

hurriedly passed over the question: "What is truth?"[47] The youth "tries to master thoughts," he "understands ideas, the spirit" and "seeks ideas"; he "is engrossed in thought," he has "absolute thoughts, i.e., nothing but thoughts, logical thoughts." The youth who thus "deports himself," instead of chasing after young women and other earthly things, is thus none other than the young Stirner,[48] the studious Berlin youth, busy with Hegel's logic and gazing with amazement at the great Michelet.[49]

Of this youth it is rightly said:

"to bring to light pure thought, to devote oneself to it — in this is the joy of youth, and all the bright images of the world of thought — truth, freedom, mankind, Man, etc. — illumine and inspire the youthful soul."

This youth then "throws aside" the "object" as well and "occupies himself" exclusively "with his thoughts":

"He includes all that is not spiritual under the contemptuous name of external things, and if, all the same, he does cling to such external things as, for example, students' customs, etc., it happens only when and because he discovers spirit in them, i.e., when they become symbols for him."

---

47 A reference to John 18:38 (*"Pilate saith unto him, What is truth? And when he had said this, he went out again unto the Jews, and saith unto them, I find in him no fault at all."*).

48 By all accounts Stirner was a quiet, solitary individual, who did not even find an intimate companion in his own wife. Engels knew him personally, as a mostly very quiet hanger-on of his Berlin Young Hegelian mates (*Die Freien* — "The Free").

49 Jules Michelet (1798-1874) was the first historian to use and define the term "Renaissance". An anti-clerical republican, he wrote a vast *History of France*.

Virtuous Berlin youth! The beer-drinking ritual[50] of the students' association was for him only a "symbol" and only for the sake of the "symbol" was he after a drinking bout many a time found under the table, where he probably also wished to "discover spirit"! — How virtuous is this good youth, is seen also from the fact that it was "made known" to him that:

"Father and mother should be abandoned, all natural authority should be considered broken."[51]

For him, "the rational man, the family as a natural authority does not exist; there follows a renunciation of parents, brothers and sisters, etc." — But they are all "re-born as *spiritual, rational* authority," thanks to which the good youth reconciles obedience and fear of one's parents with his speculating conscience, and everything remains as before. Likewise, it is said: "We ought to obey God rather than men."[52] Indeed, the good youth soon reaches the highest peak of morality, when it is said: "One should obey one's conscience rather than God." This moral exultation raises him even above the "revengeful Eumenides"[53] and

---

50 In the manuscript, Marx and Engels often make cracks which associate 'beer-drinking' with being somehow backward or philistine. Apparently, Engels and his Young Hegelian friends (which included Stirner) used to meet in a *wine bar* — presumably this was a lot cooler, back then. Nietzsche, whose scorn for his fellow Germans had even fewer bounds, would also frequently associate beer-drinking with being an old-fashioned peasant dingus.

51 Stirner was also, of course, a family abolitionist.

52 This is from Acts, 5:29.

53 The Eumenides were Greek deities of vengeance.

even above the "anger of Poseidon" — he is afraid of nothing so much as his "conscience".

Having discovered that "the spirit is the essential" he no longer even fears the following perilous conclusions: "If, however, the spirit is recognised as the essential, nevertheless it makes a difference whether the spirit is poor or rich, and therefore" (!) "one strives to become rich in spirit; the spirit wishes to expand, to establish its realm, a realm not of this world, which has just been overcome. In this way, the spirit strives to become all in all" (what way is this?) "i.e., although I am spirit, nevertheless I am not perfect spirit and must" (?) "first seek the perfect spirit."

"Nevertheless it makes a difference." — "*It*," what is this? What is the "It" that makes the difference? We shall very often come across this mysterious 'It' in our holy man, and it will then turn out that it is the unique from the standpoint of substance, the beginning of "unique" logic, and as such the true identity of Hegel's "being" and "nothing". Hence, for everything that this "It" does, says or performs, we shall lay the responsibility on our saint, whose relation to it is that of its creator. First of all, this "It", as we have seen, makes a difference between poor and rich. And why? Because: "the spirit is recognised as the essential." Poor "It", which without this recognition would never have arrived at the difference between poor and rich! "And therefore *one* strives", etc. "*One!*" We have here the second impersonal person which, together with the "It", is in Stirner's service and must perform the heaviest menial work for him. How these two are accustomed to support each other is clearly seen here. Since "It" makes a difference whether the spirit is poor or rich, "one" — "*one, therefore, strives to become rich in spirit.*" "It" gives the signal and immediately "one" joins in at the top of its voice. The division of labour is classically carried out.

Since "one strives to become *rich in spirit, the spirit* wishes to expand, to establish its *realm*," etc. "If however" a connection is present here, "it still makes a difference" whether "one" wants to become "*rich in spirit*" or whether "*the spirit* wants to establish its realm." Up to now '*the spirit*' has not wanted *anything*, '*the spirit*' has not yet figured as a person — it was only a matter of the spirit of the 'youth', and not of 'the spirit' as such, of the spirit as *subject*. But our holy writer now needs a spirit different from that of the youth, in order to place it in opposition to the latter as a foreign, and in the last resort, as a holy spirit. *Conjuring trick No. 1.*[54]

"In this way the spirit strives to become all in all" — a somewhat obscure statement, which is then explained as follows:

> "Although I am spirit, nevertheless I am not perfect spirit and must first seek the perfect spirit."

But if Saint Max is the "imperfect spirit," nevertheless it makes a difference whether he has to "*perfect*" his spirit or seek "*the perfect spirit*." A few lines earlier he was in fact dealing only with the "*poor*" and "*rich*" spirit — a quantitative, profane distinction — and now there suddenly appears the "*imperfect*" and "*perfect*" spirit — a qualitative, mysterious distinction. The striving towards the development of one's own spirit can now be transformed into the hunt of the

---

54 This section contains a number of these 'Conjuring Tricks', which Marx and Engels have identified in Stirner. The label — 'Conjuring Trick' — is in part a crack at Stirner, who is forever going on about how our 'fixed ideas' about things (the existence of 'Man', for example) are "spooks." The point, typically, is that Stirner is in truth just as egregious an idealist as the idealists he criticises.

"imperfect spirit" for "*the* perfect spirit." The holy spirit wanders about like a ghost. *Conjuring trick No. 2.*

The holy author continues:

> "But thereby I, who have only just found myself as spirit, at once lose myself again, in that bow down before the perfect spirit, as a spirit which is not my own, but a spirit of the *beyond*, and I feel my emptiness."

This is nothing but a further development of Conjuring Trick No. 2. After the "perfect spirit" has been *assumed* as an *existing being* and opposed to the "imperfect spirit," it becomes obvious that the "imperfect spirit," the youth, painfully feels his "emptiness" to the depths of his soul. Let us go on!

> "True, it is all a matter of spirit, but is every spirit the right spirit? The right and true spirit is the ideal of the spirit, the 'holy spirit'. It is not my or your spirit but precisely an ideal spirit, a spirit of the beyond — 'God'. 'God is spirit.'"

Here the "perfect spirit" has been suddenly transformed into the "right" spirit, and immediately afterwards into the "right and true spirit." The latter is more closely defined as the "ideal of the spirit, the holy spirit" and this is proved by the fact that it is "not my or your spirit but *precisely*, a spirit of the beyond, an ideal spirit — God." The true spirit is the *ideal* of the spirit, "precisely" because it is *ideal!* It is the holy spirit "precisely" because it is — God! What "virtuosity of thought"! We note also in passing that up to now nothing was said about "your" spirit. *Conjuring trick No. 3.*

Thus, if I seek to train myself as a mathematician, or, as Saint Max puts it, to "perfect" myself as a mathematician, then I am seeking the "perfect" mathematician, i.e., the "right and true" mathematician, the "ideal" of the mathematician, the "holy" mathematician, who is distinct from me and you (although in my eyes you may be a perfect mathematician, just as for the Berlin youth his professor of philosophy is the perfect spirit); but a mathematician who is "precisely ideal, of the beyond," the mathematician in the heavens, "God". God is a mathematician.

Saint Max arrives at all these great results because "it makes a difference whether the spirit is rich or poor"; i.e. — in plain language — it makes a difference whether anyone is rich or poor in spirit, and because his "youth" has discovered this remarkable fact. Saint Max continues: "It divides the man from the *youth* that the former takes the world as it is", etc.

Consequently, we do not learn how the youth arrives at the point where he suddenly takes the world "as it is", nor do we see our holy dialectician making the transition from youth to man, we merely learn that "It" has to perform this service and "*divide*" the youth from the man. But even this "It" by itself does not suffice to bring the cumbersome wagonload of unique thoughts into motion. For after "*It*" has "divided the man from the youth," the man all the same relapses again into the youth, begins to occupy himself afresh "exclusively with the spirit" and does not get going until "one" hurries to his assistance with a change of horses. "Only when one has grown fond of oneself *corporeally*, etc." — "only then" everything goes forward smoothly again, the man discovers that he has a personal interest, and arrives at "the *second self-discovery*," in that he not only "finds himself as spirit," like the youth, "and then at once loses himself again in the universal spirit," but finds himself "as *corporeal* spirit." This "corporeal spirit" finally arrives at having an "interest not only in its own spirit" (like the youth), "but in total satisfaction, in the satisfaction of the whole fellow" (an interest in the satisfaction of the whole fellow!) — he arrives at the point where "he is pleased with himself exactly as he is." Being a German, Stirner's "man" arrives at everything very late. He could see, sauntering along the Paris boulevards or in London's Regent Street, hundreds of "young men", fops and dandies who have not yet found themselves as "corporeal spirits" and are nevertheless pleased with themselves exactly as they are, and whose main interest lies precisely in the "satisfaction of the whole fellow"!

This second "self-discovery" fills our holy dialectician with such enthusiasm that he suddenly forgets his role and begins to speak not of the *man*, but of *himself*, and reveals that he himself, he the unique, is "the man," and that "the man" = "the unique." *A new conjuring trick.*

"How I find myself[55] behind the *things*, and indeed as *spirit*, so subsequently, too, I must find myself[56] behind the *thoughts*, i.e. as their creator and owner. In the period of spirits, thoughts outgrew me, although they were the offspring of my brain; like delirious fantasies they floated around me and agitated me greatly, a dreadful power. The thoughts became themselves *corporeal*, they were spectres like God, the Emperor, the Pope, the Fatherland, etc. — by destroying their corporeality, I take them back into my own corporeality and *announce*: I alone am corporeal. And now I take the world as it is for me, as my world, as my property: I relate everything to myself."

Thus, the man, identified here with the "unique", having first given thoughts corporeality, i.e., having transformed them into spectres, now destroys this corporeality again,

---

55 Marx and Engels note that this should read "how the youth finds himself."

56 Marx and Engels note that this should read "the man must find himself."

by taking them back into his own body, which he thus makes into a body of spectres. The fact that he arrives at his own corporeality only through the negation of the spectres, shows the nature of this constructed corporeality of the man, which he has first to "announce" to "himself", in order to believe in it. But *what* he announces to himself, he does not even announce correctly. The fact that apart from his "unique" body there are not also to be found in his head all kinds of independent bodies, spermatozoa, he transforms into the "*fable*": I alone am corporeal. *Another conjuring trick!*

Further, the man who, as a youth, stuffed his head with all kinds of nonsense about existing powers and relations such as the Emperor, the Fatherland, the State, etc., and knew them only as his own "delirious fantasies," in the form of his conceptions — this man, according to Saint Max, *actually destroys all these powers by getting out of his head his false opinion of them.*[57] On the contrary: now that he no longer looks at the world through the spectacles of his fantasy, he has to think of the practical interrelations of the world, to get to know them and to act in accordance with them. By destroying the fantastic corporeality which the world had for him, he finds its real corporeality outside his fantasy. With the disappearance of the *spectral* corporeality of the Emperor, what disappears for him is not the corporeality, but the *spectral character* of the Emperor, the actual power of whom he can now at last appreciate in all its scope. *Conjuring trick No. 5.*

The youth as a man does not even react critically towards ideas which are valid also for others and are current as categories, but is critical only of those ideas that are the "mere

---

57 This, of course, mirrors the more general critique of the "German Ideologists" we have already seen Marx give in my edit of the "Feuerbach" chapter above.

offspring of his brain," i.e., general concepts about existing conditions reproduced in his brain. Thus, for example, he does not even resolve the *category* "Fatherland", but only his personal opinion of this category, after which the *generally valid* category still remains, and even in the sphere of "philosophical thought" the work is only just beginning. He wants, however, to make us believe that he has destroyed the category itself because he has destroyed his emotional personal relation to it — exactly as he has wanted to make us believe that he has destroyed the power of the Emperor by giving up his fantastic conception of the Emperor. *Conjuring trick No. 6.*

"*And now,*" continues Saint Max, "I take the world as it is for me, as my world, as my property."

He takes the world as it is for him, i.e., as he is *compelled* to take it, and thereby he has *appropriated* the world for himself, has made it his property — a mode of acquisition which, indeed, is not mentioned by any of the economists, but the method and success of which will be the more brilliantly disclosed in "the book". Basically, however, he "takes" not "the world", but only his delirious *fantasy* about the world as his own, and makes it his property. He takes the world as his conception of the world, and the world as his conception is his imagined property, the property of his conception, his conception as property, his property as conception, his own peculiar conception, or his conception of property; and all this he expresses in the incomparable phrase: "I relate everything to myself."

After the man has recognised, as the saint himself admits, that the world was only populated by spectres, because the youth saw spectres, after the *illusory world* of the youth has disappeared for the man, the latter finds himself in a *real* world, independent of youthful fancies.

And so, it should therefore read: I take the world as it is *independently of myself*, in the form in which it *belongs to itself* ("the man takes the world as it is," and not as he would like it to be), in the first place as my non-property (hitherto it was my property only as a spectre). I relate myself to everything and only to that extent do I relate everything to myself.

"If I as spirit rejected the world with the deepest contempt for it, then I as proprietor reject the spectres or ideas into their emptiness. They no longer have power over me, just as no 'earthly force' has power over the spirit."

We see here that the proprietor, Stirner's man, at once enters into possession, *sine beneficio deliberandi atque inventarii*,[58] of the inheritance of the youth which, according to his own statement, consists only of "delirious fantasies" and "spectres". He believes that in the process of changing from a child into a youth he had truly coped with the world of things, and in the process of changing from a youth into a man he had truly coped with the world of the spirit, that now, as a man, he has the whole world in his pocket and has nothing more to trouble him. If, according to the words of the youth which he repeats, no earthly force outside him has any power over the spirit, and hence the spirit is the supreme power on earth — and he, the man, has forced this omnipotent spirit into subjection to himself — is he not then completely omnipotent? He forgets that he has only destroyed the fantastic and spectral form assumed by the idea of "Fatherland", etc., in the brain of the "youth", but that he has still not touched these ideas, insofar as they express actual relations. Far from having become the

---

58 "Without the advantage of deliberation or inventory" — an allusion to a right associated with inheritance law, which grants the beneficiary time to decide whether they want to accept or reject a legacy.

master of ideas — he is only now capable of arriving at "ideas".

Now, let us say in conclusion, it can be clearly seen that the holy man has brought his interpretation of the different stages of life to the desired and predestined goal. He informs us of the result achieved in a thesis that is a spectral shade which we shall now confront with its lost body.

Unique thesis: "The child was *realistic*, in thrall to the *things of this world*, until little by little he succeeded in penetrating behind these very things. The youth was *idealistic*, inspired by thoughts, until he worked his way up to become a man, the egoistic man, who deals with things and thoughts as he pleases and puts his personal interest above everything. Finally, the old man? It will be time enough to speak of this when I become one."

Owner of the accompanying liberated shade: The child was actually in thrall *to the world of his things*, until little by little (a borrowed conjuring trick standing for development) he succeeded in leaving *these very things* behind him. The youth was fanciful and was made thoughtless by his enthusiasm, until he was brought down by the man, the egoistic *burgher*, with whom things and thoughts deal as they please, because his personal interest puts everything above him. Finally, the old man? — "Woman, what have I to do with thee?"[59]

The entire history of "a man's life" amounts, therefore, *let us say in conclusion,* to the following:

(1) Stirner regards the various stages of life only as "self-discoveries" of the individual, and these "self-discoveries"

_____

59 Marx and Engels here allude to John 2:4 (Jesus is talking to Mary).

are moreover always reduced to a definite relation of *consciousness*. Thus the variety of consciousness is here the life of the individual. The physical and social changes which take place in the individuals and produce an altered consciousness are, of course, of no concern to Stirner. In Stirner's work, therefore, child, youth and man always find the world ready-made, just as they merely "find" "themselves"; absolutely nothing is done to ensure that there should be something which can in fact be found. But even the relation of *consciousness* is not correctly understood either, but only in its speculative distortion. Hence, too, all these figures have a philosophical attitude to the world — "the child is *realistic*," "the youth is *idealistic*," the man is the negative unity of the two, absolute negativity, as is evident from the above-quoted final proposition. Here the secret of "a man's life" is revealed, here it becomes clear that the "*child*" was only a disguise of "*realism*", the "*youth*" a disguise of "*idealism*", the "*man*" of an attempted solution of this *philosophical antithesis*. This solution, this "*absolute negativity*", is arrived at — it is now seen — only thanks to the man blindly taking on trust the illusions both of the child and of the youth, *believing* thus to have overcome the world of things and the world of the spirit.

(2) Since Saint Max pays no attention to the physical and social "life" of the individual, and says nothing at all about "life", he quite consistently abstracts from historical epochs, nationalities, classes, etc., or, which is the *same thing*, he inflates the *consciousness* predominant in the class nearest to him in his immediate environment into the normal consciousness of "a man's life". In order to rise above this local and pedantic narrow-mindedness he has only to confront "his" youth with the first young clerk he encounters, a young English factory worker or young Yankee, not to mention the young Kirghiz-Kazakhs.

(3) Our saint's enormous gullibility — the true spirit of his book — is not content with causing his youth to believe in his child, and his man to believe in his youth. The illusions which some "youths", "men", etc., have or claim to have about themselves, are without any examination accepted by Stirner himself and confused with the *"life"*, with the *reality*, of these highly ambiguous youths and men.

(4) The prototype of the entire structure of the stages of life has already been depicted in the third part of Hegel's *Encyclopedia* and "in various transformations" in other passages in Hegel as well.[60] Saint Max, pursuing "his own" purposes, had, of course, to undertake certain "transformations" here also. Whereas Hegel, for example, is still to such an extent guided by the empirical world that he portrays the German burgher as the servant of the world around him, Stirner has to make him the master of this world, which he is not even in imagination. Similarly, Saint Max pretends that he does not speak of the old man for empirical reasons; he wishes to wait until he becomes one himself (here, therefore, "a man's life" = his unique life). Hegel briskly sets about constructing the four stages of the human life because, in the real world, the negation is posited twice, i.e. as moon and as comet (cf. Hegel's *Philosophy of Nature*), and therefore the quaternity here takes the place of the trinity. Stirner finds his own uniqueness in making moon and comet coincide and so abolishes the unfortunate old man from "a man's life".[61] The

---

60 The third part of Hegel's *Encyclopedia of the Philosophical Sciences* is concerned with *"Geist"* (that is: "Spirit", or "Mind" — the thing that his *Phenomenology* is a "Phenomenology" of).

61 At one point in the "Sankt Max" document, Marx and Engels comment that "The difference between 'Stirner' and Hegel is that the former achieves the same things without the help of

reason for this conjuring trick becomes evident as soon as we examine the construction of the unique history of man.

The Economy of the Old Testament

We must here, for a moment, jump from the "Law" to the "Prophets", since at this point already we reveal the secret of unique domestic economy in heaven and on earth. In the Old Testament, too — where the law, man, still is a schoolmaster of the unique — the history of the kingdom of the unique follows a wise plan fixed from eternity. Everything has been foreseen and preordained in order that the unique could appear in the world, when the time had come to redeem holy people from their holiness.

The first book, "A Man's Life", is also called the "Book of Genesis", because it contains in embryo the entire domestic economy of the unique, because it gives us a prototype of the whole subsequent development up to the moment when the time comes for the end of the world. The entire unique history revolves round three stages: child, youth and man, who return "in various transformations" and in ever widening circles until, finally, the entire history of the world of things and the world of the spirit is reduced to "child, youth and man". Everywhere we shall find nothing but disguised "child, youth and man", just as we already discovered in them three disguised categories.

We spoke above of the German philosophical conception of history. Here, in Saint Max, we find a brilliant example of it. The speculative idea, the abstract conception, is

---

dialectics." In a way, I can think of no better reason to stop talking about Hegel in relation to Marx, really at all. If you can get to the same (wrong) place without taking on the immense metaphysical (and practical) burden of the Hegelian system and his method, why bothering taking the long way round?

made the driving force of history, and history is thereby turned into the mere history of philosophy. But even the latter is not conceived as, according to existing sources, it actually took place — not to mention how it evolved under the influence of real historical relations — but as it was understood and described by recent German philosophers, in particular Hegel and Feuerbach. And from these descriptions again only that was selected which could be adapted to the given end, and which came into the hands of our saint by tradition. Thus, history becomes a mere history of illusory ideas, a history of spirits and ghosts, while the real, empirical history that forms the basis of this ghostly history is only utilised to provide bodies for these ghosts; from it are borrowed the names required to clothe these ghosts with the appearance of reality. In making this experiment our saint frequently forgets his role and writes an undisguised ghost-story.

In his case we find this method of making history in its most naive, most classic simplicity. Three simple categories — realism, idealism and absolute negativity (here named "egoism") as the unity of the two — which we have already encountered in the shape of the child, youth and man, are made the basis of all history and are embellished with various historical signboards; together with their modest suite of auxiliary categories they form the content of all the allegedly historical phases which are trotted out. Saint Max once again reveals here his boundless faith by pushing to greater extremes than any of his predecessors' faith in the speculative content of history dished up by German philosophers. In this solemn and tedious construction of history, therefore, all that matters is to find a pompous series of resounding names for three categories that are so hackneyed that they no longer dare to show themselves publicly under their own names. Our anointed author could perfectly well have passed from the "man" at the start of the book immediately to the "ego" in the middle, or better still to the "unique" at the very end; but that would have been too simple. Moreover, the strong competition among the German speculative philosophers makes it the duty of each new competitor to offer an ear-splitting historical advertisement for his commodity.[62]

The Free Ones[63]

A. Political Liberalism

The key to the criticism of liberalism advanced by Saint Max and his predecessors is the history of the German bourgeoisie. We shall call special attention to some aspects of this history since the French Revolution.

The state of affairs in Germany at the end of the last century is fully reflected in Kant's *Critique of Practical Reason*. While the French bourgeoisie, by means of the most colossal revolution that history has ever known, was

---

62 At this point in the manuscript, Marx and Engels provide a detailed analysis of the architectonic of Stirner's work. Their critique then proceeds by going through this architectonic piece-by-piece. In short, having noted that Stirner wastes a lot of time by not proceeding directly from man to "the ego" and then to "the unique", they decide to wilfully commit the same sin. In this abridgement, obviously, I have been determined not to follow them: we skip instead to the next bit of their critique that will actually be of interest to people who are not primarily interested in Stirner, namely Marx and Engels's critique of Stirner's critique of "political liberalism".

63 This subheading corresponds to the relevant section in Stirner's book. As well as "Political Liberalism" and "Social Liberalism" (Communism), there is also a section on "Humane Liberalism" — I have not included Marx and Engels's response to that here.

achieving domination and conquering the continent of Europe, while the already politically emancipated English bourgeoisie was revolutionising industry and subjugating India politically, and all the rest of the world commercially, the impotent German burghers did not get any further than "good will". Kant was satisfied with "good will" alone, even if it remained entirely without result, and he transferred the *realisation* of this good will, the harmony between it and the needs and impulses of individuals, to *the world beyond*.[64] Kant's good will fully corresponds to the impotence, depression and wretchedness of the German burghers, whose petty interests were never capable of developing into the common, national interests of a class and who were, therefore, constantly exploited by the bourgeois of all other nations. These petty, local interests had as their counterpart, on the one hand, the truly local and provincial narrow-mindedness of the German burghers and, on the other hand, their cosmopolitan swollen-headedness. In general, from the time of the Reformation German development has borne a completely petty-bourgeois character. The old feudal aristocracy was, for the most part, annihilated in the peasant wars; what remained of it were either imperial petty princes who gradually achieved a certain independence and aped the absolute monarchy on a minute, provincial scale, or lesser landowners who partly squandered their little

---

64 In Kantian ethics, you're basically supposed to need the idea of the afterlife in order to be motivated to act well at all, since even if you do what you're "supposed" to (act in line with the categorical imperative), the evil of others means you're unlikely to secure even a minimally decent outcome (see, for instance, the famous example where a crazed murderer appears at your doorstep and asks where your family are: Kant's ethics demands that you not lie to him).

bit of property at the tiny courts, and then gained their livelihood from petty positions in the small armies and government offices — or, finally, Junkers from the backwoods, who lived a life of which even the most modest English *squire* or French *gentilhomme de province* would have been ashamed. Agriculture was carried on by a method which was neither parcellation nor large-scale production, and which, despite the preservation of feudal dependence and corvées, never drove the peasants to seek emancipation, both because this method of farming did not allow the emergence of any active revolutionary class and because of the absence of the revolutionary bourgeoisie corresponding to such a peasant class.

As regards the middle class, we can only emphasise here a few significant factors. It is significant that linen manufacture, i.e., an industry based on the spinning wheel and the hand-loom, came to be of some importance in Germany at the very time when in England those cumbersome tools were already being ousted by machines. Most characteristic of all is the position of the German middle class in relation to *Holland*. Holland, the only part of the Hanseatic League that became commercially important, tore itself free, cut Germany off from world trade except for two ports (Hamburg and Bremen) and since then dominated the whole of German trade. The German middle class was too impotent to set limits to exploitation by the Dutch. The bourgeoisie of little Holland, with its well-developed class interests, was more powerful than the far more numerous German middle class with its indifference and its divided petty interests. The fragmentation of interests was matched by the fragmentation of political organisation, the division into small principalities and free imperial cities. How could political concentration arise in a country which lacked all the economic conditions for it?

The impotence of each separate sphere of life (one can speak here neither of estates nor of classes, but at most of former estates and classes not yet born) did not allow any one of them to gain exclusive domination. The inevitable consequence was that during the epoch of absolute monarchy, which assumed here its most stunted, semi-patriarchal form, the special sphere which, owing to division of labour, was responsible for the administration of public interests acquired an abnormal independence, which became still greater in the bureaucracy of modern times. Thus, the state built itself up into an apparently independent force, and this position, which in other countries was only transitory — a transition stage — it has maintained in Germany until the present day. This position of the state explains both the conscientiousness of the civil servant, which is found nowhere else, and all the illusions about the state which are current in Germany, as well as the apparent independence of German theoreticians in relation to the middle class — the seeming contradiction between the form in which these theoreticians express the interests of the middle class and these interests themselves.

The characteristic form which French liberalism, based on real class interests, assumed in Germany we find again in Kant. Neither he, nor the German middle class, whose whitewashing spokesman he was, noticed that these theoretical ideas of the bourgeoisie had as their basis material interests and a *will* that was conditioned and determined by the material relations of production. Kant, therefore, separated this theoretical expression from the interests which it expressed; he made the materially motivated determinations of the will of the French bourgeois into pure self-determinations of "*free will*", of the will in and for itself, of the human will, and so converted it into purely ideological conceptual determinations and moral postulates. Hence the German petty bourgeois recoiled in horror from the practice of this energetic bourgeois liberalism as soon as this practice showed itself, both in the Reign of Terror and in shameless bourgeois profit-making.

Under the rule of Napoleon, the German middle class pushed its petty trade and its great illusions still further. As regards the petty-trading spirit which predominated in Germany at that time, Saint Sancho[65] can, *inter alia*, compare Jean Paul, to mention only works of fiction, since they are the only source open to him. The German citizens, who railed against Napoleon for compelling them to drink chicory and for disturbing their peace with military billeting and recruiting of conscripts, reserved all their moral indignation for Napoleon and all their admiration for England; yet Napoleon rendered them the greatest services by cleaning out Germany's Augean stables[66] and establishing civilised means of communication, whereas the English only waited for the opportunity to exploit them *à tort et à travers*.[67] In the same petty-bourgeois spirit the German princes imagined they were fighting for the principle of legitimism and against revolution, whereas they

---

65 That is, Stirner. I've deleted most of this stuff because to be honest, the joke doesn't really land, but throughout "Sankt Max", Marx and Engels frequently compare Stirner to Sancho Panza, with another member of the Young Hegelian circle, a minor theorist and later ultra-conservative military officer named Szeliga, cast as Don Quixote. The joke, broadly speaking, is that Stirner only looks like any sort of "realist" whatsoever in comparison to his utterly deluded idealistic companions.

66 "Cleaning the Augean Stables" was one of the Labours of Heracles — King Augeas had a massive stables containing thousands of cattle, which hadn't been cleaned in over thirty years, so you can see why cleaning them would be impressive.

67 We would say, "without rhyme or reason."

were only the paid mercenaries of the English bourgeoisie. In the atmosphere of these universal illusions it was quite in the order of things that the estates privileged to cherish illusions — ideologists, school-masters, students, members of the *Tugendbund*[68] — should talk big and give a suitable high-flown expression to the universal mood of fantasy and indifference. The political forms corresponding to a developed bourgeoisie were passed on to the Germans from outside by the July revolution[69] — as we mention only a few main points we omit the intermediary period. Since German economic relations had by no means reached the stage of development to which these political forms corresponded, the middle class accepted them merely as abstract ideas, principles valid in and for themselves, pious wishes and phrases, Kantian self-determinations of the will and of human beings as they ought to be. Consequently their attitude to these forms was far more moral and disinterested than that of other nations, i.e., they exhibited a highly peculiar narrow-mindedness and remained unsuccessful in all their endeavours.

Finally the ever more powerful foreign competition and world intercourse — from which it became less and less possible for Germany to stand aside — compelled the diverse local interests in Germany to adopt some sort of common attitude. Particularly since 1840, the German

---

68 The "League of Virtue" — a quasi-Masonic secret society, established to revive the national spirit of the Prussians after their defeat by Napoleon.

69 The French revolution of 1830, which led to the overthrow of the anti-liberal restoration monarch Charles X. He was replaced by a constitutional monarchy led by his cousin Louis-Philippe. In Hegel's *Philosophy of Right*, a constitutional monarchy is also the political form that is ultimately aimed at (by history, or whatever).

middle class began to think about safeguarding these common interests; its attitude became national and liberal and it demanded protective tariffs and constitutions. Thus it has now got almost as far as the French bourgeoisie in 1789.

If, like the Berlin ideologists, one judges liberalism and the state within the framework of local German impressions, or limits oneself merely to criticism of German-bourgeois illusions about liberalism, instead of seeing the correlation of liberalism with the real interests from which it originated and without which it cannot really exist — then, of course, one arrives at the most banal conclusions. This German liberalism, in the form in which it expressed itself up to the most recent period, is, as we have seen, even in its popular form, empty enthusiasm, ideological reflections about *real* liberalism.[70] How easy it is, therefore, to transform its content wholly into philosophy, into pure conceptual determinations, into "rational cognition"! Hence if one is so unfortunate as to know even this bourgeoisified liberalism only in the sublimated form given it by Hegel and the school-masters who depend on him, then one will arrive at conclusions belonging exclusively to the sphere of the holy. Sancho will provide us with a pitiful example of this.

---

70 Another point at which the text seems to be very presciently describing how things are today, where the most enthusiastic defenders of "liberalism" are, all-too-often, precisely those most willing to capitulate to the people determined to destroy it. See academic controversies over "freedom of speech", in a context where universities — especially those lower down the academic food chain — are being forced to make substantial cuts to the humanities. These defenders of "liberalism" love to get distracted by meaningless debates over abstract principle, appearing to have little interest in — or even, conception of — political reality.

Recently, in active circles, so much has been said about the rule of the bourgeois, that it is not surprising that news of it has even penetrated to Berlin, and there attracted the attention of easy-going school-masters.[71] It cannot, however, be said that "Stirner" in his method of appropriating current ideas has adopted a particularly fruitful and profitable style — as was already evident from his exploitation of Hegel and will now be further exemplified.

It has not escaped our school-master that in recent times the liberals have been identified with the bourgeois. Since Saint Max identifies the bourgeois with the good burghers, with the petty German burghers, he does not grasp what has been transmitted to him as it is in fact and as it is expressed by all competent authors — viz., that the liberal phrases are the idealistic expression of the real interests of the bourgeoisie — but, on the contrary, as meaning that the final goal of the bourgeois is to become a perfect liberal, a citizen of the state. For Saint Max the bourgeois is not the truth of the *citoyen*, but the *citoyen* the truth of the bourgeois. This conception, which is as holy as it is German, goes to such lengths that "the middle class" (it should read: "the domination of the bourgeoisie") is transformed into a "thought, nothing but a thought" and "the state" comes forward as the "true man", who in the "Rights of Man" confers the rights of "Man", the true solemnisation on each individual bourgeois. Hence he can transform the bourgeois — having separated the bourgeois as a liberal from the empirical bourgeois — into a holy liberal, just as he transforms the state into the "holy", and the relation of the bourgeois to the modern state into a holy relation, into a cult — and with this, in effect, he concludes his criticism of political liberalism. He has transformed it into the "holy".

---

71 Stirner, again, is the school-master in question.

We wish to give here a few examples of how Saint Max embellishes this property of his with historical arabesques. For this purpose he uses the French Revolution, concerning which a small contract to supply him with a few data has been negotiated by his history-broker, Saint Bruno.

On the basis of a few words from Bailly,[72] obtained moreover through the intermediary of Saint Bruno's memory,[73] the statement is made that through the convening of the Estates General "those who hitherto were subjects arrive at the consciousness that they are proprietors." On the contrary, *mon brave*! By the convening of the Estates General, those who hitherto were proprietors show their consciousness of being no longer subjects: a consciousness which was long ago arrived at, for example in the Physiocrats, and — in polemical form against the bourgeoisie — in Linguet, Mercier, Mably, and, in general, in the writings against the Physiocrats.[74] This meaning was also immediately understood at the beginning of the revolution — for example by Brissot, Fauchet, Marat, in the *Cercle social* and by all the democratic opponents of Lafayette. If Saint Max had understood the matter as it took place independently of his history-broker, he would not have been surprised that "Bailly's words certainly *sound* as if each man were now a proprietor," and that the

---

72 Jean-Sylvain Bailly (1736-93), mayor of Paris in the early years of the French Revolution (later guillotined during the Terror).

73 The reference here is actually to an essay by Bruno Bauer's brother Edgar, "Bailly and the First Days of the French Revolution", in *Memories of Recent History Since the Revolution*, by Bruno and Edgar Bauer.

74 "Physiocracy" was an Enlightenment-era economic theory which held that the "wealth of nations" was derived solely from the value of agricultural land.

bourgeois "express... the rule of the proprietors... that now the proprietors have become the bourgeoisie *par excellence*."

The "statement of the Bishop of Autun and Barère" that Stirner refers to is a *motion* tabled on July 4 (not 8).[75] It was carried on July 9, hence it is not at all clear why Saint Max speaks of "July 8".[76] This motion by no means "destroyed" "the illusion that each man, the individual, was of importance", etc. — but it destroyed the binding force of the *Cahiers* given to the deputies, that is, the influence and the "importance," not of "each man, the individual," but

---

75 That is: Talleyrand (1754-1838), the endlessly cunning and cynical diplomat who served in turn the *Ancien Régime*, the Revolution, Bonaparte, the Bourbon Restoration, and the July Monarchy. Appointed to his Bishopric shortly before the Revolution, he later supported the anti-clericalism of the revolutionaries, and resigned after being excommunicated in 1791.

76 The motion in question reads: "The National Assembly, considering that a *bailliage* or portion of a *bailliage* has the right to form only the general will, and not to evade it, or to suspend the activity of the Estates General by imperative mandates, which contain only a particular will, declares that all imperative mandates are radically void, that the kind of engagement which resulted from them must be promptly lifted by the *bailliages*, as such a clause could not be imposed, all protestations to the contrary being inadmissible, and that by a necessary consequence, all decrees of the National Assembly will be rendered obligatory on every *bailliage*, when it has been made by all without exception." (from Robert H. Blackman, *1789: The French Revolution Begins*). Incidentally, Blackman appears to contradict Marx and Engels, giving July 8 as the date when the issue the motion is concerned with was indeed "resolved."

of the feudal 177 *bailliages* and 431 *divisions des ordres*.[77]
By carrying the motion, the Assembly discarded the
characteristic features of the old, feudal *États généraux*.[78]
Moreover, it was at that time by no means a question of
the correct theory of popular representation, but of highly
practical, essential problems.

Broglie's army held Paris at bay and drew nearer every
day; the capital was in a state of utmost agitation; hardly a
fortnight had passed since the *jeu de paume*[79] and the *lit de
justice*, the court was plotting with the bulk of the aristocracy
and the clergy against the National Assembly; lastly, owing
to the still existing feudal provincial tariff barriers, and as a
result of the feudal agrarian system as a whole, most of the
provinces were in the grip of famine and there was a great
scarcity of money. At that moment it was a question of an
assemblée essentiellement active, as Talleyrand himself put it,
while the *Cahiers* of [the] aristocratic and other reactionary
groups provided the court with an opportunity to declare
[the] decision of the Assembly [void by referring] to the
wishes of the constituents. The Assembly proclaimed its
independence by carrying Talleyrand's motion and seized
the power it required, which in the political sphere could, of
course, only be done within the framework of political form
and by making use of the existing theories of Rousseau, etc.
The National Assembly had to take this step because it was
being urged forward by the immense mass of the people

---

77 The *Cahiers de doléances*, the 'Lists of Grievances' drawn up by
    the three Estates (Clergy, Nobility, and "Everyone Else"), which
    were put before the king in March and April 1789.

78 In short, by reversing the polarity from *bailliages* binding the
    Assembly, to the Assembly being able to bind the *bailliages*.

79 "*Jeu de Paume*", i.e. what we would call "real tennis". The reference
    here is to the "Tennis Court Oath", with which the Third Estate
    signified their united opposition to the king.

that stood behind it. By so doing, therefore, it did not at all transform itself into an "utterly egoistical chamber, completely cut off from the umbilical cord and ruthless"; on the contrary it actually transformed itself thereby into the *true organ* of the vast majority of Frenchmen, who would otherwise have crushed it, as they later crushed "utterly egoistical" deputies who "completely cut themselves off from the umbilical cord." But Saint Max, with the help of his history-broker, sees here merely the solution of a theoretical question; he takes the Constituent Assembly, six days before the storming of the Bastille, for a council of church fathers debating a point of dogma! The question regarding the "importance of each man, the individual", can, moreover, only arise in a democratically elected representative body, and during the revolution it only came up for discussion in the Convention, and for as empirical reasons as earlier the question of the *Cahiers*. A problem which the Constituent Assembly decided *also* theoretically was the distinction between the representative body of a ruling class and that of the ruling estates; and this political rule of the bourgeois class was determined by each individual's position, since it was determined by the relations of production prevailing at the time. The representative system is a very specific product of modern bourgeois society which is as inseparable from the latter as is the isolated individual of modern times.

Just as here Saint Max takes the 177 *bailliages* and 431 *divisions des ordres* for "individuals", so he later sees in the absolute monarch and his *car tel est notre plaisir*[80] the rule of the 'individual' as against the constitutional monarch, the "rule of the apparition" — and in the aristocrat and the guild-member he again sees the "individual" in contrast to the citizen.

---

80 "For this is our will" — the words which customarily closed royal edicts.

"The Revolution was not directed against reality, but against this reality, against this definite existence."

"Stirner" thinks it makes no difference to the "good burghers and their principles," whether an absolute or a constitutional king, a republic, etc. — For the "good burghers" who quietly drink their beer in a Berlin beer-cellar this undoubtedly "makes no difference"; but for the historical bourgeois it was by no means a matter of indifference. The "good burgher" "Stirner" here again imagines that the French, American and English bourgeois are good Berlin beer-drinking philistines. If one translates the sentence above from the language of political illusion into plain language, it means: "it makes no difference" to the bourgeoisie whether it rules unrestrictedly or whether its political and economic power is counterbalanced by other classes. Saint Max believes that an absolute king, or someone else, could defend the bourgeoisie just as successfully as it defends itself. And even "its principles," which consist in subordinating state power to *"chacun pour soi, chacun chez soi"*[81] and exploiting it for that purpose — an "absolute monarch" is supposed to be able to do that! Let Saint Max name any country with developed trade and industry and strong competition where the bourgeoisie entrusts its defence to an "absolute monarch".

After this transformation of the historical bourgeois into German philistines devoid of history, "Stirner", of course, does not need to know any other bourgeois than "comfortable burghers and loyal officials" — two spectres who only dare to show themselves on "holy" German soil — and can lump together the whole class as "obedient servants." Let him just take a look at these obedient servants on the stock exchanges of London, Manchester,

81 "Every man for himself."

New York, and Paris. Since Saint Max is well under way, he can now go the whole hog and, believing one of the narrow-minded theoreticians of the *Einundzwanzig Bogen* who says that "liberalism is rational cognition applied to our existing conditions," can declare that the "liberals are fighters for reason."[82] It is evident from these phrases how little the Germans have recovered from their original illusions about liberalism. Abraham "against hope believed in hope," and his faith "was imputed to him for righteousness."[83]

> "The state pays well, so that its good citizens can without danger pay poorly; it provides itself by means of good payment with servants from whom it forms a force — the police — for the protection of good citizens and the good citizens willingly pay high taxes to the state in order to pay so much lower amounts to their workers."

This should read: the bourgeois pay their state well and make the nation pay for it so that without risk they should be able to pay poorly; by good payment they ensure that the state servants are a force available for their protection — the police; they willingly pay, and force the nation to pay high taxes so as to be able without danger to shift the sums they pay on to the workers as a levy (as a deduction from wages). "Stirner" here makes the new economic discovery that wages are a levy, a tax, paid by the bourgeois to the proletarian; whereas the other, mundane economists regard taxes as a tribute which the proletarian pays to the bourgeois.

---

82 From an article entitled "Preussen seit der Einsetzung Arndt's bis zur Absetzung Bauers", published anonymously in the *Einundzwanzig Bogen aus der Schweiz*.

83 Romans 4: 18-22.

Our holy church father now passes from the holy middle class to the Stirnerian "unique" proletariat. The latter consists of "rogues, prostitutes, thieves, robbers and murderers, gamblers, propertyless people with no occupation and frivolous individuals." They form the "dangerous proletariat" and for a moment are reduced by "Stirner" to "individual shouters," and then, finally, to "vagabonds," who find their perfect expression in the "spiritual vagabonds" who do not "keep within the bounds of a moderate way of thinking."

"So wide a meaning has the so-called proletariat or pauperism!"

"On the other hand, the state sucks the life-blood" of the proletariat. Hence the entire proletariat consists of ruined bourgeois and ruined proletarians, of a collection of ragamuffins, who have existed in every epoch and whose existence on a mass scale after the decline of the Middle Ages preceded the mass formation of the ordinary proletariat, as Saint Max can ascertain by a perusal of English and French legislation and literature. Our saint has exactly the same notion of the proletariat as the "good comfortable burghers" and, particularly, the "loyal officials". He is consistent also in identifying the proletariat with pauperism, whereas pauperism is the position only of the ruined proletariat, the lowest level to which the proletarian sinks who has become incapable of resisting the pressure of the bourgeoisie, and it is only the proletarian whose whole energy has been sapped who becomes a pauper. Compare Sismondi, Wade, etc.[84] "Stirner" and his fraternity, for example, can in the

---

84 Simonde de Sismondi (1773-1842), pioneering liberal critic of laissez-faire economics; John Wade (1788-1875), leader writer

eyes of the proletarians, in certain circumstances count as paupers but never as proletarians.

Such are Saint Max's "own" ideas about the bourgeoisie and the proletariat. But since with these imaginations about liberalism, good burghers and vagabonds he, of course, gets nowhere, he finds himself compelled in order to make the transition to communism to bring in the actual, ordinary bourgeois and proletarians insofar as he knows about them from hearsay. Thus the lumpen-proletariat are transformed into "workers," into ordinary proletarians, while the bourgeois "in course of time" undergoes "occasionally" a series of "various transformations" and "manifold refractions." In one line we read: "*The propertied rule*," i.e., the profane bourgeois; six lines later we read: "The citizen is what he is by the grace of the state," i.e., the holy bourgeois; yet another six lines later: "The state is the status of the middle class," i.e., the profane bourgeois; this is then explained by saying that "the state gives the propertied... their property in feudal possession," and that the "money and property" of the "capitalists," i.e., the holy bourgeois, is such "state property" transferred by the state to "feudal possession." Finally, this omnipotent state is again transformed into the "state of the propertied," i.e., of the profane bourgeois, which is in accord with a later passage: "Owing to the revolution the bourgeoisie became omnipotent." Even Saint Max would never have been able to achieve these "heart-rending" and "horrible" contradictions — at any rate, he would never have dared to promulgate them — had he not had the assistance of the German word "*Bürger*"[85], which he can interpret at will as "*citoyen*" or as "*bourgeois*" or as the German "good burgher."

---

for *The Spectator* and author of *The History of the Middle and Working Classes* (1833).

85 That is: "citizen".

Before going further, we must take note of two more great politico-economic discoveries which our simpleton "brings into being" "in the depths of his heart" and which have in common with the "joy of youth" the feature of being also "pure thoughts."

All the evil of the existing social relations is reduced to the fact that "burghers and workers believe in the 'truth' of money." *Jacques le Bonhomme*[86] imagines that it is in the power of the "burghers" and "workers", who are scattered among all civilised states of the world, suddenly, one fine day, to put on record their "disbelief" in the "truth of money"; he even believes that if this nonsense were possible, something would be achieved by it. He believes that any Berlin writer could abolish the "truth of money" with the same ease as he abolishes in his mind the "truth" of God or of Hegelian philosophy. That money is a necessary product of definite relations of production and intercourse and remains a "truth" so long as these relations exist — this, of course, is of no concern to a holy man like Saint Max, who raises his eyes towards heaven and turns his profane backside to the profane world.[87]

The second discovery amounts to this, that "the worker cannot turn his labour to account" because he "falls into the hands" of "those who" have received "some kind of

---

86 Marx and Engels occasionally give Stirner the nickname "Jacques le Bonhomme" ("Jack Goodfellow"). Said Jack was the presumed leader of the "Jacquerie", a peasant revolt in fourteenth-century France. (Presumably, then, the idea is to deride Stirner as somehow historically backwards or vulgar — as with the other "Germans", his is a medieval thought in a modern age.)

87 Compare contemporary political commentators who honestly believe that if the Israelis and the Palestinians were to simply abandon their respective religions, all conflict in the region would immediately cease.

state property... in feudal possession." This is merely a further explanation of the sentence already quoted above where the state sucks the life-blood of the worker. And here everyone will immediately "put forward" "the simple reflection" — that "Stirner" does not do so is not "surprising" — how does it come about that the state has not given the "workers" also some sort of "state property" in "feudal possession." If Saint Max had asked himself this question he would probably have managed to do without his construction of the "holy" burghers, because he would have been bound to see the relation in which the propertied stand to the modern state.

By means of the opposition of the bourgeoisie and proletariat — as even "Stirner" knows — one arrives at communism. But how one arrives at it, *only* "Stirner" knows.

> "The workers have the most tremendous power in their hands... they have only to cease work and to regard what they have produced by their labour as their property and to enjoy it. This is the meaning of the workers' disturbances which flare up here and there."

Workers' disturbances, which even under the Byzantine Emperor Zeno led to the promulgation of a law, which "flared up" in the fourteenth century in the form of the Jacquerie[88] and Wat Tyler's rebellion, in 1518 on the Evil May Day in London, and in 1549 in the great uprising of the tanner Kett, and later gave rise to Act 15 of the second and third year of the reign of Edward VI, and a series of similar Acts of Parliament; the disturbances which soon afterwards, in 1640 and 1659 (eight uprisings in one year), took place in Paris and which already since the fourteenth century must have been frequent in France and England,

---

88 See n. 86 above.

judging by the legislation of the time; the constant war which since 1770 in England and since the revolution in France has been waged with might and cunning by the workers against the bourgeoisie — all this exists for Saint Max only "here and there," in Silesia, Poznan, Magdeburg and Berlin, "according to German newspaper reports." What is produced by labour, according to the imagination of *Jacques le Bonhomme*, would continue to exist and be reproduced, as an object to be "regarded" and "enjoyed," even if the producers "ceased work."

As he did earlier in the case of money, now again our good burgher transforms "the workers," who are scattered throughout the civilised world, into a private club which has only to adopt a decision in order to get rid of all difficulties. Saint Max does not know, of course, that at least fifty attempts have been made in England since 1830, and at the present moment yet another is being made, to gather all the English workers into a single association and that highly empirical causes have frustrated the success of all these projects. He does not know that even a minority of workers who combine and go on strike very soon find themselves compelled to act in a revolutionary way — a fact he could have learned from the 1842 uprising in England and from the earlier Welsh uprising of 1839, in which year the revolutionary excitement among the workers first found comprehensive expression in the 'sacred month,' which was proclaimed simultaneously with a general arming of the people.

Here again we see how Saint Max constantly tries to pass off his nonsense as "*the* meaning" of historical facts (in which he is successful at best in relation to *his* "one") — historical facts "on which he foists his own meaning, which are thus bound to lead to nonsense." Incidentally, it would never enter the head of any proletarian to turn to Saint Max for advice about the "meaning" of the proletarian movements or what should be undertaken at the present time against the bourgeoisie.

After this great campaign, our Saint Sancho returns to his Maritornes[89] with the following fanfare:

"The state rests on the *slavery of labour*. If *labour* were to become *free*, the state would be lost".

The *modern* state, the rule of the bourgeoisie, is based on *freedom of labour*.[90] The idea that along with freedom of religion, state, thought, etc., and hence "occasionally" "also" "perhaps" with freedom of *labour*, not I become free, but only one of my enslavers — this idea was borrowed by Saint Max himself, many times, though in a very distorted form, from the *Deutsch-Französische Jahrbücher*. Freedom of labour is free competition of the workers among themselves. Saint Max is very unfortunate in political economy as in all *other* spheres. Labour *is* free in all civilised countries; it is not a matter of freeing labour but of abolishing it.[91]

B. Communism

Saint Max calls communism "social liberalism," because he is well aware how great is the disrepute of the word liberalism among the radicals of 1842 and the most advanced Berlin "free-thinkers".[92] This transformation gives him at the same time the opportunity and courage to put into the mouths

---

89 This is another reference to Don Quixote. Maritornes is a half-blind servant girl Quixote encounters at an inn. She shelters under Sancho's blanket during a brawl.

90 In contrast with the feudal state, which really is based on indentured labour.

91 See n. 34 above.

92 Clearly, on this point, nothing has changed.

of the "social liberals" all sorts of things which had never been uttered before "Stirner" and the refutation of which is intended to serve also as a refutation of *communism*.

Communism is overcome by means of a series of partly logical and partly historical constructions.[93]

First Logical Construction

"'Because we have seen ourselves made into servants of egoists, we should not ourselves become egoists... but should rather see to it that egoists become impossible. We want to turn them all into ragamuffins, we want no one to possess anything, in order that 'all' should be possessors.' — So say the social liberals. Who is this person whom you call 'all'? It is 'society'?"

With the aid of a few quotation marks Sancho here transforms "all" into a person, society as a person, as a subject = holy society, the holy. Now our saint knows what he is about and can let loose the whole torrent of his flaming anger against "the holy", as the result of which, of course, communism is annihilated.

---

93 In this abridgement I've only included the logical constructions, with a little bit of material from the "historical constructions" worked in at the end. In my view the historical constructions do not, in themselves, add much to the critique overall. In large part this is because, while Stirner (obviously) likes a big sweeping idealised historical narrative as much as the next nineteenth-century German thinker, his "history" is so thin that it barely adds anything to his argument at all. So, ultimately, all that Marx and Engels's critique of the "historical constructions" really does, is end up leaving this section of the text feeling repetitive and overlong.

That Saint Max here again puts his nonsense into the mouth of the "social liberals", as being the meaning of their words, is not surprising. He identifies first of all "owning" as a private property-owner with "owning" in general. Instead of examining the definite relations between private property and production, instead of examining "owning" as a landed proprietor, as a rentier, as a merchant, as a factory-owner, as a worker — where "owning" would be found to be a quite distinct kind of owning, control over other people's labour — he transforms all these relations into "owning as such."

Second Logical Construction

Political liberalism made the "nation" the supreme owner. Hence communism has no longer to "abolish" any "personal property" but, at most, has to equalise the distribution of "feudal possessions", to introduce *égalité* there.

Saint Sancho here takes as communism the ideas of a few liberals tending towards communism, and the mode of expression of some communists who, for very practical reasons, express themselves in a political form.

After "Stirner" has transferred property to "society", all the members of this society in his eyes at once become paupers and ragamuffins, although — even according to his idea of the communist order of things — they "own" the "supreme owner".

His benevolent proposal to the communists — "to transform the word 'ragamuffin' into an honourable form of address, just as the revolution did with the word 'citizen'" — is a striking example of how he confuses communism with something which long ago passed away.[94] The revolution even

---

94 Stirner's conception of communism perhaps looks at least somewhat like the "really existing communism" of, e.g., the

"transformed" the word *sans culotte* "into an honourable form of address," as against "*honnêtes gens*", which he translates very inadequately as "good citizens".

Saint Sancho notes that the "elevation of society to supreme owner" is a "second *robbery* of the personal element in the interests of humanity," while communism is only the completed robbery of the "robbery of the personal element." "Since he unquestionably regards robbery as detestable," Saint Sancho "therefore believes for example," that he "has branded" communism "already by the" above "proposition". Once "Stirner" has detected "even robbery" in communism, how could he fail to feel "profound disgust" at it and "just indignation"? We now challenge "Stirner" to name a bourgeois who has written about communism (or Chartism) and has not put forward the same absurdity with great emphasis. Communism will certainly carry out "robbery" of what the bourgeois regards as "personal".[95]

First Corollary

"Liberalism at once came forward with the statement that it is an essential feature of man to be not property, but property-owner. Since it was a question here of man,

---

Soviet Union under Josef Stalin. Presumably, the contemporary equivalent to the sort of fallacy Stirner is committing here would be, you know, someone who says that communism or socialism have 'failed' as such, simply because the Soviet state happened to collapse.

95 This line is echoed in *The Communist Manifesto*. "The distinguishing feature of Communism is not the abolition of property generally, but the abolition of bourgeois property... Hard-won, self-acquired, self-earned property?... There is no need to abolish that; the development of industry has to a great extent already destroyed it, and is still destroying it daily."

and not of an individual, the question of how much, which was precisely what constituted the particular interest of individuals, was left to their discretion. Therefore, the egoism of individuals had the widest scope as regards this how much and carried on tireless competition."

That is to say: liberalism, i.e., liberal private property-owners, at the beginning of the French Revolution, gave private property a liberal appearance by declaring it one of the rights of man. They were forced to do so if only because of their position as a revolutionising party; they were even compelled not only to give the mass of the French rural population the right to property, but also to let them *seize actual property*, and they could do all this because thereby their own "how much?", which was what chiefly interested them, remained intact and was even made safe.

We find here further that Saint Max makes competition arise from liberalism, a slap that he gives history in revenge for the slaps which he had to give himself above. A "more exact explanation" of the manifesto with which he makes liberalism "*at once* come forward" can be found in Hegel, who in 1820 expressed himself as follows:

"In respect of external things it is rational that I should possess property... what and how much I possess is, therefore, legally a matter of chance" (*Philosophy of Right*, §49).

It is characteristic of Hegel that he turns the phrase of the bourgeois into the true concept, into the essence of property, and "Stirner" faithfully imitates him. On the basis of the above analysis, Saint Max now makes the further statement, that communism:

"... raised the question as to how much property, and answered it in the sense that man should have as much as he needs. Can my egoism be satisfied with that?... No. I must rather have as much as I am capable of appropriating."

First of all it should be remarked here that communism has by no means originated from §49 of the *Philosophy of Right* and its "what and how much?" Secondly, "communism" does not dream of wanting to give anything to "Man", for "communism" is not at all of the opinion that "Man" "needs" anything apart from a brief critical elucidation.[96] Thirdly, Stirner foists on to communism the conception of "need" held by the present-day bourgeois; hence he introduces a distinction which, on account of its paltriness, can be of importance only in present-day society and its ideal copy — Stirner's union of "individual shouters" and free seamstresses. "Stirner" has again achieved great "penetration" into the essence of communism.

Finally, in his demand to have as much as he is capable of appropriating (if this is not the usual bourgeois phrase that everyone should have as much as his ability permits him, that everyone should have the right of free gain), Saint Sancho assumes communism as having already been achieved in order to be able freely to develop his "ability" and put it into operation, which by no means depends solely on him, any more than his fortune itself, but depends also on the relations of production and intercourse in which he lives. Incidentally, even Saint Max himself does not behave according to his doctrine, for throughout his "book" he "needs" things and uses things which he was not "capable of appropriating".

---

96 Cf. the discussion already staged in ns. 14 and 40 above.

Second Corollary

"But the social reformers preach a social law to us. The individual thus becomes the slave of society... In the opinion of the communists, everyone should enjoy the eternal rights of man."

As far as law is concerned, we with many others have stressed the opposition of communism to law, both political and private, as also in its most general form as the rights of man. See the *Deutsch-Französische Jahrbücher*, where privilege, the special right, is considered as something corresponding to private property inseparable from social classes, and law as something corresponding to the state of competition, of free private property; equally, the rights of man themselves are considered as privilege, and private property as monopoly. Further, criticism of law is brought into connection with German philosophy and presented as the consequence of criticism of religion; further, it is expressly stated that the legal axioms that are supposed to lead to communism are axioms of private property, and the right of common ownership is an imaginary premise of the right of private property. Incidentally, even in the works of German communists passages appeared very early — e.g., in the writings of Hess[97] — which could be appropriated and distorted by "Stirner" in his criticism of law.

Incidentally, the idea of using the phrase quoted above against Babeuf,[98] of regarding him as the theoretical

---

97 Moses Hess (1812-1875), early communist and Zionist philosopher. A friend of Marx and Engels's during the 1840s, he worked on a chapter of what was to be *The German Ideology*, but also found himself critiqued in it.

98 François-Noël Babeuf (1760-1797), French proto-socialist writer of the Revolutionary period. The word "communism"

representative of communism could only occur to a Berlin school-master. "Stirner", however, has the effrontery to assert that:

> "Communism, which assumes that all people by nature have equal rights, refutes its own thesis and asserts that people by nature have no rights at all. For it does not want, for example, to admit that parents have rights in relation to their children; it abolishes the family.[99] In general, this whole revolutionary or Babouvist principle is based on a religious, i.e., false, outlook."

A Yankee comes to England, where he is prevented by a Justice of the Peace from flogging his slave, and he exclaims indignantly: "Do you call this a land of liberty, where a man can't larrup his nigger?"

Saint Sancho here makes himself doubly ridiculous. Firstly, he sees an abolition of the "equal rights of man" in the recognition of the "equal rights by nature" of children in relation to parents, in the granting of the *same* rights of man to children as well as to parents. Secondly, two pages previously *Jacques le bonhomme* tells us that the state does not interfere when a father beats his son, because it recognises family rights. Thus, what he presents, on the one hand, as a particular right (family right), he includes, on the other hand, among the "equal rights of man by nature." Finally, he admits that he knows Babeuf only

---

was first used in English to describe his followers. Presumably there is a sort of *QI*-logic at work in Stirner here: identifying the thing itself with whatever it first happened to be (I remember one episode of *QI*, for instance, where Stephen Fry confidently declared that the national colour of Ireland was "blue," on the basis that some old Irish flag happened to be blue).

99 See n. 19 above.

from the Bluntschli report,[100] while this report, in turn, admits that its wisdom is derived from the worthy L. Stein, Doctor of Law.[101] Saint Sancho's thorough knowledge of communism is evident from this quotation. Just as Saint Bruno is his broker as regards revolution, so Saint Bluntschli is his broker as regards communists. With such a state of affairs we ought not to be surprised that a few lines lower down our rustic word of God reduces the *fraternité* of the revolution to "equality of the children of God" (in what Christian dogma is there any talk of *égalité*?).

Third Corollary

Because the principle of community culminates in communism, therefore: communism = "apotheosis of the state founded on love."

From the state founded on love, which is Saint Max's own fabrication, he here derives communism which then, of course, remains an exclusively Stirnerian communism. Saint Sancho knows only egoism on the one hand or the claim to the loving services, pity and alms of people on the other hand. Outside and above this dilemma nothing exists for him at all.[102]

---

100 A text by one Johann Caspar Bluntschli (1808-1881) entitled *The Communists in Switzerland*.

101 Lorenz von Stein (1815-1890), author of *Socialism and Communism in Contemporary France*.

102 Here we see Marx and Engels deal with another perennial fallacy with regard to Communism: the idea that people would not be somehow "moral" enough for it, that they are simply "too selfish" or whatever. For Marx and Engels, Communism will be founded not on love or selflessness or anything noble like that, but on simple necessity — on want, and desire. At

Third Logical Construction

> "Since the most oppressive evils are to be observed in society, it is especially the oppressed who think that the blame is to be found in society and set themselves the task of discovering the right society."

On the contrary, it is "Stirner" who "sets himself the task" of discovering the "society" which is "right" for *him*, the holy society, the society as the incarnation of the holy. Those who are "oppressed" nowadays "in society", "think" only about how to achieve the society which is *right for them*, and this consists primarily in abolishing the present society on the basis of the existing productive forces. If, e.g., "oppressive evils are to be observed" in a machine — if, for example, it refuses to work, and those who need the machine (for example, in order to make money) find the fault in the machine and try to alter it, etc. — then, in Saint Sancho's opinion, they are setting themselves the task not of putting the machine *right*, but of discovering the right machine, the holy machine, the machine as the incarnation of the holy, the holy as a machine, the machine in the heavens.[103] "Stirner" advises them to seek the blame "*in themselves*." Is it not their fault that, for example, they need a hoe and a plough? Could they not use their bare

---

the heart of their thought is a deep anti-moralism. See also Introduction.

103 As we have already seen, Marx and Engels state in the "Feuerbach" chapter: "Communism is for us not a *state of affairs* which is to be established, an ideal to which reality will have to adjust itself. We call communism the *real* movement which abolishes the present state of things." For Marx and Engels, you have gotten communism exactly wrong if you conceive of it as some heavenly quest for some "holy machine".

hands to plant potatoes and to extract them from the soil afterwards?[104] The saint preaches to them as follows:

> "It is merely an ancient phenomenon that one seeks first of all to lay the blame anywhere but on oneself — and therefore on the state, on the selfishness of the rich, for which, however, we ourselves are to blame."

The "oppressed" who seeks to lay the "blame" for pauperism on the "state" is, as we have noted above, no other than *Jacques le bonhomme* himself. Secondly, the "oppressed" who comforts himself by causing the "blame" to be laid on the "selfishness of the rich" is again no other than *Jacques le bonhomme*. And, thirdly, who is the person that should bear the "blame"? Is it, perhaps, the proletarian child who comes into the world tainted with scrofula, who is reared with the help of opium and is sent into the factory when seven years old; is it the individual worker who is here expected to 'revolt' by himself against the world market; or is it, perhaps, the girl who must either starve or become a prostitute? No, not these but only he who seeks "all the blame", i.e., the "blame" for everything in the present state of the world, "in himself", viz., once again no other than *Jacques le bonhomme* himself. "This is merely the ancient phenomenon" of Christian heart-searching and doing penitence in a German-speculative form, with its idealist phraseology, according to which I, the actual man, do not have to change actuality, which I can only change together with others, but have to change myself in myself.

According to Saint Sancho, therefore, those oppressed by society seek the right society. If he were consistent, he should make those who "seek to lay the blame on the

---

104 At this point Marx and Engels appear to be describing Stirner as Dwight from the US *Office*.

state" — and according to him they are the very same people — also seek the right state. But he cannot do this, because he has heard that the communists want to abolish the state. He has now to construct this abolition of the state, and our Saint Sancho once more achieves this with the aid of his "donkey", the apposition, in a way that "looks very simple":

> "Since the workers are in a state of distress, the existing state of affairs, i.e., the state, must be abolished."

What could "look simpler"? "It is only surprising" that the English bourgeois in 1688 and the French in 1789 did not "put forward" the same "simple reflections" and equations. It follows from this that wherever a "state of distress" exists, "the State", which is, of course, the same in Prussia and North America, must be abolished.

As is his custom, Saint Sancho now presents us with a few proverbs of Solomon.[105]

Proverb of Solomon No. 1

> "That society is no ego, which could give, etc., but an instrument from which we can derive benefit; that we have no social duties, but only interests; that we do not owe any sacrifices to society, but if we do sacrifice something we sacrifice it for ourselves — all this is disregarded by the social liberals, because they are in thrall to the religious principle and are zealously striving for a — holy society."

The following "penetrations" into the essence of communism result from this:

---

105 I'm not completely sure why Marx and Engels label them this; probably just to keep with the text's low-key overall "biblical" theme.

(1) Saint Sancho has quite forgotten that it was he himself who transformed "society" into an "ego" and that consequently he finds himself only in his own "society".

(2) He believes that the communists are only waiting for "society" to "give" them something, whereas at most they want to give themselves a society.

(3) He transforms society, even before it exists, into an instrument from which he wants to derive benefit, without him and other people by their mutual social relations creating a society, and hence this "instrument".

(4) He believes that in communist society there can be a question of "duties" and "interests", of two complementary aspects of an antithesis which exists only in bourgeois society (under the guise of interest the reflecting bourgeois always inserts a third thing between himself and his mode of action — a habit seen in truly classic form in Bentham, whose nose had to have some interest before it would decide to smell anything. Compare "the book" on the right to one's nose).

(5) Saint Max believes that the communists want to "make sacrifices" for "society", when they want at most to sacrifice existing society; in this case he should describe their consciousness that their struggle is the common cause of all people who have outgrown the bourgeois system as a sacrifice that they make to themselves.

(6) That the social liberals are in thrall to the religious principle.

(7) That they are striving for a holy society — these points have already been dealt with above. How "zealously" Saint

Sancho "strives" for a "holy society", so as to be able to refute communism by means of it, we have already seen.

Proverb of Solomon No. 2

"If interest in the social problem were less passionate and blind, then one… would understand that a society cannot be turned into a new one so long as those of whom it consists *and* who constitute it remain as of old."

"Stirner" believes that the communist proletarians who revolutionise society and put the relations of production and the form of intercourse on a new basis — i.e., on themselves as new people, on their new mode of life — that these proletarians remain "as of old". The tireless propaganda carried on by these proletarians, their daily discussions among themselves, sufficiently prove how little they themselves want to remain "as of old", and how little they want people to remain "as of old".[106] They would only remain "as of old" if, with Saint Sancho, they "sought the blame in themselves"[107]; but they know too well that only under changed circumstances will they cease to be "as of old", and therefore they are determined to change these circumstances at the first opportunity. In revolutionary activity the changing of oneself coincides with the changing of circumstances. This great saying is explained by means of an equally great example which, of course, is again taken from the world of "the holy".

Saint Max calmly utters the great historic words:

"Human beings, by no means intending to achieve their own development, have always wanted to form a society."

---

106 Nowadays this seems somewhat optimistic.
107 This, on the other hand, seems exactly right.

Human beings, by no means wanting to form a society, have, nevertheless, only achieved the development of society, because they have always wanted to develop only as isolated individuals and therefore achieved their own development only in and through society. Incidentally it would only occur to a saint of the type of our Sancho to separate the development of "human beings" from the development of the "society" in which they live, and then let his fantasy roam on this fantastic basis. Incidentally, he has forgotten his own proposition, inspired by Saint Bruno, in which just previously he set people the moral demand of changing themselves and thereby changing their society — a proposition, therefore, in which he identifies the development of people with the development of their society.[108]

Fourth Logical Construction

Stirner makes the communists say, in opposition to the citizens:

"Our essence does not consist in all of us being equal children of the state, but in that we all exist for one another. We are all equal in that we all exist for one another, that each works for the other, that each of us is a worker."

---

108 In a similar vein, at one point in the "historical constructions" part of the manuscript, Marx and Engels comment (sarcastically): "Man" must become a master! — "Man" remains a maker of pin-heads, but he has the consolation of knowing that the pin-head is part of the pin and that he *is able* to make the whole pin. The fatigue and disgust caused by the eternally repeated making of pin-heads is transformed, by this knowledge, into the "satisfaction of man".

He then regards "to exist as a worker" as equivalent to "each of us exists only through the other," so that the other, "for example, works to clothe me, and I to satisfy his need of entertainment, he for my food and I for his instruction. Hence participation in labour is our dignity and our equality."

"What advantage do we derive from citizenship? Burdens. And what value is put on our labour? The lowest possible ... What can you put against us? Again, only labour! Only for labour do we owe you a recompense; only for what you do that is useful to us... have you any claim on us. We want to be only worth so much to you as we perform for you; but you should be valued by us in just the same way. Deeds which are of some value to us, i.e., work beneficial to the community, determine value... He who does something useful takes second place to no one, or — all workers (beneficial to the community) are equal. Since however the worker is worthy of his wage, then let the wage also be equal."

With "Stirner", "communism" begins with searchings for "essence"; being a good "youth" he wants again only to "penetrate behind things." That communism is a highly practical movement, pursuing practical aims by practical means, and that only perhaps in Germany, in opposing the German philosophers, can it spare a moment for the problem of "essence" — this, of course, is of no concern to our saint. This Stirnerian "communism", which yearns so much for "essence", arrives, therefore, only at a philosophical category, i.e., "being-for-one-another", which then by means of a few arbitrary equations:

Being-for-one-another = to exist *only* through another
= to exist as a worker
= universal community of workers

... is brought somewhat closer to the empirical world. We would, moreover, challenge Saint Sancho to indicate, for example, in Owen (who, after all, as a representative of English communism can serve as an example of "communism" just as well as, for example, the non-communist Proudhon, from whom the greater part of the above propositions were abstracted and then rearranged) a passage containing anything of these propositions about "essence", universal community of workers, etc. Incidentally we do not even have to go so far back. The third issue of *Die Stimme des Volks*, the German communist magazine, says:

"What is today called labour is only a miserably small part of the vast, mighty process of production; for *religion* and *morality* honour with the name of *labour* only the kind of production that is repulsive and dangerous, and in addition they venture to embellish such labour with all kinds of maxims — as it were words of blessing (or witchcraft) — 'labour in the sweat of thy brow' as a test imposed by God; 'labour sweetens life' for encouragement, etc. The morality of the world in which we live takes very good care not to apply the term work to the pleasing and free aspects of human intercourse. These aspects are reviled by morality, although they too constitute production. Morality eagerly reviles them as vanity, vain pleasure, sensuality. Communism has exposed this hypocritical preaching, this miserable morality."

As universal community of workers, Saint Max reduces the whole of communism to equal wages. "Against competition," Stirner states, "there rises the principle of the society of ragamuffins — *distribution*. Is it possible then," Stirner asks, "that I, who am very resourceful, should have no advantage over one who is resourceless?" Further, he speaks of a "universal tax on human activity in communist society." Finally, he ascribes to the communists the view that "labour" is "the only resource" of man. Thus, Saint Max re-introduces into communism private property in its dual form — as distribution and wage-labour. As before in connection with "robbery", Saint Max here again displays the most ordinary and narrow-minded bourgeois views as 'his own' 'penetrations' into the essence of communism. As a real petty bourgeois, he is then afraid that he, "who is very resourceful... should have no advantage over one who is resourceless" — although he *should* fear nothing so much as being left to his own "resources".

Incidentally, he "who is very resourceful" imagines that citizenship is a matter of indifference to the proletarians, after he has first assumed that they *have* it. This is just as he imagined above that for the bourgeoisie the form of government is a matter of indifference. The workers attach so much importance to citizenship, i.e., to *active* citizenship, that where they have it, for instance in America, they "make good use" of it, and where they do not *have* it, they strive to obtain it. Compare the proceedings of the North American workers at innumerable meetings, the whole history of English Chartism, and of French communism and reformism.[109]

---

109 Marx and Engels make an important point here about the psychologies of worker's movements, which are not typically attempting to establish some "ideal", but rather to make certain definite, concrete demands. Organised labour does not seek what it *ought* — that is, *because* it ought to — but what it *can* — because it is powerful enough to.

First Corollary

"The worker, being conscious that the essential thing about him is that he is a worker, keeps himself away from egoism and subordinates himself to the supremacy of a society of workers, just as the bourgeois adhered with devotion to the state based on competition."

The worker is at most conscious that for the bourgeois the essential thing about him is that he is a worker, who, therefore, can assert himself against the bourgeois as such. Both these discoveries of Saint Sancho, the "devotion of the bourgeois" and the "*state* based on competition", can be recorded only as fresh proofs of the "resourcefulness" of the "very resourceful" man.

Second Corollary

"The aim of communism is supposed to be the 'well-being of all'. This indeed really looks as though in this way no one need be in an inferior position. But what sort of well-being will this be? Have all one and the same well-being? Do all people feel equally well in one and the same circumstances? If that is so, then it is a matter of 'true well-being'. Does we not thereby arrive precisely at the point where the tyranny of religion begins? Society has decreed that a particular sort of well-being is 'true well-being', and if this well-being were, for example, *honestly earned enjoyment*, but you preferred enjoyable idleness, then society would prudently refrain from making provision for what is for you the rule of the holy, hierarchy... well-being. By proclaiming the well-being of all, communism destroys the well-being of those who up to now have lived as rentiers, etc."

"If that is so", the following equations result from it:

The well-being of all = Communism
                  = If that is so
                  = One and the same well-being of all
                  = Equal well-being of all in one and the same circumstances
                  = True well-being
                  = Holy well-being, the holy, the rule of the holy, hierarchy
                  = Tyranny of religion.

Thus:

Communism = Tyranny of religion.

This indeed really looks as though "Stirner" has said the same thing about communism as he has said previously about everything else.

How deeply our saint has "penetrated" into the essence of communism is evident also from the fact that he ascribes to communism the desire to bring about "true well-being" in the shape of "honestly earned enjoyment". Who, except "Stirner" and a few Berlin cobblers and tailors, thinks of "honestly earned enjoyment"?! Who, except "Stirner", is able to attribute such moral absurdities to the immoral revolutionary proletarians, who, as the whole civilised world knows (Berlin, of course, does not belong to the civilised world), have the wicked intention not "honestly to earn" their "enjoyment" but to take it by conquest!

And, what is more, to put this into the mouth of communists, for whom the basis of this whole opposition between work and enjoyment disappears. Let our highly moral saint put his mind at rest on this score. "Honest earning" will be left to him and those whom, unknown to himself, he represents — his petty handicraftsmen who have been ruined by industrial freedom and are morally "indignant". "Enjoyable idleness", too, belongs wholly to the most trivial bourgeois outlook.[110] But the crowning point of the whole statement is the artful bourgeois scruple that he raises against the communists: that they want to abolish the "well-being" of the rentier and yet talk about the "well-being of all".[111] Consequently, he believes that in communist society there will still be rentiers, whose "well-being" would have to be abolished. He asserts that "well-being" *as rentier* is inherent in the individuals who are at present rentiers, that it is inseparable from their individuality, and he imagines that for these individuals there can exist no other "well-being" than that which is determined by their position as rentiers.

He believes further that a society which has still to wage a struggle against rentiers and the like, is already organised in a communist way. And finally he makes the moral demand that the communists should quietly allow themselves to be exploited to all eternity by rentiers, merchants, factory-owners, etc., because they cannot abolish this exploitation without at the same time destroying the "well-being" of these gentlemen. *Jacques le bonhomme*, who poses here as the champion of the gros-bourgeois, can save himself the trouble of preaching moralising sermons to the communists, who can every day hear much better ones from his "good burghers". The communists, at any rate, will have no scruples about overthrowing the rule of the bourgeoisie and abolishing its "well-being", as soon as they are strong enough to do so. It does not matter to them at all whether this "well-being" common to their enemies and determined by class relations also appeals as personal "well-being" to a sentimentality which is narrow-mindedly presumed to exist. The "well-being" which the rentier enjoys as rentier

---

110 Sorry, Fully Automated Luxury Communists!
111 Truly, landlords have Never Changed.

is not the "well-being" of the individual as such, but of the rentier, not an individual well-being but a well-being that is general within the framework of the class.

When the narrow-minded bourgeois says to the communists: by abolishing property, i.e., my existence as a capitalist, as a landed proprietor, as a factory-owner, and your existence as workers, you abolish my individuality and your own; by making it impossible for me to exploit you, the workers, to rake in my profit, interest or rent, you make it impossible for me to exist as an individual.[112] — When, therefore, the bourgeois tells the communists: by abolishing my existence as a *bourgeois*, you abolish my existence as an *individual*; when thus he identifies himself as a bourgeois with himself as an individual, one must, at least, recognise his frankness and shamelessness. For the bourgeois it is actually the case, he believes himself to be an individual only insofar as he is a bourgeois.[113]

But when the theoreticians of the bourgeoisie come forward and give a general expression to this assertion, when they equate the bourgeois's property with individuality in theory as well and want to give a logical justification for this equation, then this nonsense begins to become solemn and holy.

Stirner's arguments regarding the impossibility of abolishing private property depend on his transforming private property into the concept of property, on exploiting the etymological connection between the words *property* [*Eigentum*] and *own* [*eigen*] and declaring the word *own* an

---

112 This paragraph and the following are taken from the "historical constructions" section, but in my view they fit only awkwardly there, and much better here.

113 Compare also the likes of Lord Alan Sugar — the archetypal "extravagantly wealthy man who still believes himself, by dint of his origins, to be the salt of the earth".

eternal truth, because even under the communist system it could happen that a stomach-ache will be *own* to him. All this theoretical nonsense, which seeks refuge in etymology, would be impossible if the actual private property that the communists want to abolish had not been transformed into the abstract notion of "property". This transformation, on the one hand, saves one the trouble of having to say anything, or even merely to know anything, about actual private property and, on the other hand, makes it easy to discover a contradiction in communism, since *after* the abolition of (*actual*) property it is, of course, easy to discover all sorts of things in communism which can be included in the concept "property".

In reality, of course, the situation is just the reverse. Actual private property is something extremely general which has nothing at all to do with individuality, which indeed directly nullifies individuality. Insofar as I am regarded as a property-owner I am not regarded as an individual — a statement which is corroborated every day by the marriages for money. In reality I possess private property only insofar as I have something vendible, whereas what is *peculiar* to me may not be vendible at all. My frock-coat is private property for me only so long as I can barter, pawn or sell it, so long as it is marketable. If it loses that feature, if it becomes tattered, it can still have a number of features which make it valuable *for me*, it may even become a feature of me and turn me into a tatterdemalion.[114] But no economist would think of classing it as my private property, since it does not enable me to command any, even the smallest, amount of other people's labour. A lawyer, an ideologist of private property, could perhaps still indulge in

---

114 Someone who goes around in tattered clothing (probably nowadays Marx and Engels would have made a slightly outmoded remark about hipsters).

such twaddle. Private property *alienates* the individuality not only of people but also of things. Land has nothing to do with rent of land, the machine has nothing to do with profit. For the landed proprietor, land has the significance only of rent of land; he leases his plots of land and receives rent; this is a feature which land can lose without losing a single one of its inherent features, without, for example, losing any part of its fertility; it is a feature the extent and even the existence of which depends on social relations which are created and destroyed without the assistance of individual landed proprietors. It is the same with machines.

In a word, rent of land, profit, etc., these actual forms of existence of private property, are *social relations* corresponding to a definite stage of production, and they are "*individual*" only so long as they have not become fetters on the existing productive forces.

Third Corollary

In communist society, Stirner tells us:

"worry arises again in the form of labour."

The good citizen "Stirner", who is already rejoicing that he will again find his beloved "worry" in communism, has nevertheless miscalculated this time. "Worry" is nothing but the mood of oppression and anxiety which in the middle class is the necessary companion of labour, of beggarly activity for securing scanty earnings. "Worry" flourishes in its purest form among the German good burghers, where it is chronic and "always identical with itself", miserable and contemptible, whereas the poverty of the proletarian assumes an acute, sharp form, drives him into a life-and-death struggle, makes him a revolutionary, and therefore engenders not "worry", but passion. If then communism wants to abolish both the "worry" of the burgher and the poverty of the proletarian, it goes without saying that it cannot do this without abolishing the cause of both, i.e., "labour".

Conclusion

Saint Sancho, as we have seen, takes delight in turning the proletarians — and hence also the communists — into "ragamuffins". He defines his "ragamuffin" as a "man possessing only ideal wealth." If Stirner's "ragamuffins" ever set up a vagabond kingdom, as the Paris beggars did in the fifteenth century,[115] then Saint Sancho will be the vagabond king, for he is the "perfect" ragamuffin, a man possessing not even ideal wealth and therefore living on the interest from the capital of his opinion. Having thus done away with the real basis of communism, i.e., the *definite* conjuncture of conditions under the bourgeois regime, he can now also transform this airy communism into his holy communism.[116]

The New Testament: "Ego"

Whereas in the Old Testament the object of our edification was "unique" logic in the framework of the past, we are now confronted by the present time in the framework of "unique" logic. We have already thrown sufficient light on

---

115 This appears to be a reference to the so-called "*Cour des miracles*" (Court of Miracles) — the slum districts of Paris, which were often thought to have developed a counter-society containing institutions devoted to the regulation of begging, thievery, etc.

116 See n. 41 above. For Marx and Engels, again, the point is that the proletariat either are, or will be, *actually powerful enough*, under bourgeois society, to overthrow it.

the "unique" in his manifold antediluvian "refractions" — as man, Caucasian, perfect Christian, truth of humane liberalism, negative unity of realism and idealism, etc. Along with the historical construction of the "ego", the "ego" itself also collapses. This "ego", the end of the historical construction, is no "corporeal" ego, carnally procreated by man and woman, which needs no construction in order to exist; it is an "ego" spiritually created by two categories, "idealism" and "realism", a merely conceptual existence.[117]

The Phenomenology of the Egoist in Agreement with Himself[118]

(i)

Saint Sancho's true egoist in agreement with himself must on no account be confused with the trivial, everyday egoist, the "egoist in the ordinary sense." Rather he has as his presupposition both this latter (the one in thrall to

---

117 Whereas the "Old Testament" section of the "Sankt Max" manuscript critiques the first part of Stirner's book (on "Man"), the "New Testament" section critiques the second part ("I" — that is "*Ich*", the Ego).

118 The notion of an egoist "in agreement with himself" makes perfect, intuitive sense if you've spent a lot of time reading and engaging with German Idealist philosophy — but if you haven't, it probably doesn't. Basically: in Hegel and Hegel-associated philosophy, things are forever striving to become somehow "aligned", or "in agreement with", their own concept — to *really be* (actually, finally, *permanently be*, with all those potentially change-driving internal contradictions ironed out) the thing that they are. The egoist "in agreement with himself" would thus be both a *true* egoist (whatever being a "true egoist" means), and know it.

the world of things, child, Negro, ancient, etc.) and the selfless egoist (the one in thrall to the world of thoughts, youth, Mongol, modern, etc.). It is, however, part of the nature of the secrets of the unique that this antithesis and the negative unity which follows from it — the *egoist in agreement with himself* — can be examined only now, in the New Testament.

Since Saint Max wishes to present the "true egoist" as something quite new, as the goal of all preceding history, he must, on the one hand, prove to the selfless, the advocates of *dévoûment*[119], that they are egoists against their will, and he must prove to the egoists in the ordinary sense that they are selfless, that they are not true, holy, egoists.

Let us begin with the first, with the selfless. We have already seen countless times that in the world of *Jacques le bonhomme* everyone is obsessed by the holy. "Nevertheless it makes a difference" whether "one is educated or uneducated." The educated, who are occupied with pure thought, confront us here as "obsessed" by the holy *par excellence*. They are the "selfless" in their practical guise.

> "Who then is selfless? Completely most likely he who stakes everything else on one thing, one aim, one purpose, one passion… He is ruled by a passion to which he sacrifices all others. And are these selfless not selfish, perhaps? Since they possess only a single ruling passion, they are concerned only with a single satisfaction, but the more ardently on that account. All their deeds and actions are egoistic, but it is a one-sided, concealed, narrow egoism; it is — obsession."

Hence, according to Saint Sancho, they possess only a single ruling passion; ought they to be concerned also

---

119 "Devotion."

with the passions which not they, but others possess, in order to rise to an all-round, unconcealed, unrestricted egoism, in order to correspond to this alien scale of "holy" egoism?

In this passage are incidentally introduced also the "miser" and the "pleasure-seeker" (probably because Stirner thinks that he seeks "pleasure" as such — holy pleasure — and not all sorts of real pleasures), as also "Robespierre, for example, Saint-Just, and so on"[120] as examples of "selfless, obsessed egoists." "From a certain moral point of view it is argued" (i.e., our holy "egoist in agreement with himself" argues from his own point of view in extreme disagreement with himself) "approximately as follows":

> "But if I sacrifice other passions to one passion, I still do not thereby sacrifice myself to this passion, and I do not sacrifice anything thanks to which I am truly I myself."

Saint Max is compelled by these two propositions "in disagreement with each other" to make the "paltry" distinction that one may well sacrifice six "for example," or seven, "and so on", passions to a single other passion without ceasing to be "truly I myself", but by no means ten passions, or a still greater number. Of course, neither Robespierre nor Saint-Just was "truly I myself", just as neither was truly "man", but they were truly Robespierre and Saint-Just, those unique, incomparable individuals.

The trick of proving to the "selfless" that they are egoists is an old dodge, sufficiently exploited already by Helvetius

---

120 Maximilien Robespierre (1758-1794), head of the Committee of Public Safety (and thus architect of the Reign of Terror); Louise Antoine de Saint-Just (1767-1794), often known as "the Angel of Death", close ally of Robespierre.

and Bentham.[121] Saint Sancho's "own" trick consists in the transformation of "egoists in the ordinary sense" — the bourgeois — into non-egoists. Helvetius and Bentham, at any rate, prove to the bourgeois that by their narrow-mindedness they in practice harm themselves, but Saint Max's "own" trick consists in proving that they do not correspond to the "ideal", the "concept", the "essence", the "calling", etc., of the egoist and that their attitude towards themselves is not that of absolute negation. Here again he has in mind only his German petty bourgeois.

This second class of the hitherto existing egoists is defined as follows:

> "These people [the bourgeois] are therefore not selfless, not inspired, not ideal, not consistent, not enthusiasts; they are egoists in the ordinary sense, selfish people, thinking of their own advantage, sober, calculating, etc."

Since "the book" is not all of a piece, we have already had occasion to see how Stirner achieves the trick of transforming the bourgeois into non-egoists, chiefly owing to his great ignorance of real people and conditions. This same ignorance serves him here as a lever.

> "This [i.e., Stirner's fantasy about unselfishness] is repugnant to the stubborn brain of worldly man but for thousands of years he at least succumbed so far that he had to bend his obstinate neck and worship higher powers... [The egoists in the ordinary sense] behave half clerically and half in a worldly way, they serve both God and Mammon."

---

121 I think Nietzsche pulls a similar trick somewhere too (the old "altruism is motivated by self-interest, because people enjoy being altruistic" thing).

"The Mammon of heaven and the God of the world both demand precisely the same degree of self-denial" — hence it is impossible to understand how self-denial for Mammon and self-denial for God can be opposed to each other as "worldly" and "clerical."

> "How does it happen, then, that the egoism of those who assert their personal interest nevertheless constantly succumbs to a clerical or school-masterly, i.e., an ideal, interest?"

It happens because:

> "Their personality seems to them too small, too unimportant — as indeed it is — to lay claim to everything and be able to assert itself fully. A sure sign of this is the fact that they divide themselves into two persons, an eternal and a temporal; on Sundays they take care of the eternal aspect and on weekdays the temporal. They have the priest within them, therefore they cannot get rid of him."

Sancho experiences some scruples here; he asks anxiously whether "the same thing will happen" to peculiarity, the egoism in the extraordinary sense.

We shall see that it is not without grounds that this anxious question is asked. Before the cock has crowed twice, Saint Jacob (*Jacques le bonhomme*) will have "denied" himself thrice.[122]

He discovers to his great displeasure that the two sides prominently appearing in history, the private interest of individuals and the so-called general interest, always

---

122 Have to admit I'm a bit baffled why Stirner is suddenly "Saint Jacob" here. The "denied himself" bit is presumably another reference to the gospels (Mark 8:34).

accompany each other. As usual, he discovers this in a false form, in its holy form, from the aspect of ideal interests, of the holy, of illusion. He asks: how is it that the ordinary egoists, the representatives of personal interests, are at the same time dominated by general interests, by school-masters, by the hierarchy? His reply to the question is to the effect that the bourgeois, etc., "seem to themselves too small", and he discovers a "sure sign" of this in the fact that they behave in a religious way, i.e., that their personality is divided into a temporal and an eternal one, that is to say, he explains their religious behaviour by their religious behaviour, after first transforming the struggle between general and personal interests into a mirror image of the struggle, into a simple reflection inside religious fantasy.

If Sancho's question is translated from its high-flown form into everyday language, then it now reads: How is it that personal interests always develop, against the will of individuals, into class interests, into common interests which acquire independent existence in relation to the individual persons, and in their independence assume the form of general interests? How is it that as such they come into contradiction with the actual individuals and in this contradiction, by which they are defined as general interests, they can be conceived by consciousness as ideal and even as religious, holy interests? How is it that in this process of private interests acquiring independent existence as class interests the personal behaviour of the individual is bound to be objectified, estranged, and at the same time exists as a power independent of him and without him, created by intercourse, and is transformed into social relations, into a series of powers which determine and subordinate the individual, and which, therefore, appear in the imagination as 'holy' powers?

Had Sancho understood the fact that within the framework of definite *modes of production*, which, of course, are not dependent on the will, alien practical forces, which are independent not only of isolated individuals but even of all of them together, always come to stand above people — then he could be fairly indifferent as to whether this fact is presented in a religious form or distorted in the fancy of the egoist, above whom everything is placed in imagination, in such a way that he places nothing above himself. Sancho would then have descended from the realm of speculation into the realm of reality, from what people fancy to what they actually are, from what they imagine to how they act and are bound to act in definite circumstances. What seems to him a product of *thought*, he would have understood to be a product of *life*. He would not then have arrived at the absurdity worthy of him — of explaining the division between personal and general interests by saying that people imagine this division also in a religious way and *seem* to themselves to be such and such, which is, however, only another word for "imagining".

Incidentally, even in the banal, petty-bourgeois German form in which Sancho perceives the contradiction of personal and general interests, he should have realised that individuals have always started out from themselves, and could not do otherwise, and that therefore the two aspects he noted are aspects of the personal development of individuals; both are equally engendered by the empirical conditions under which the individuals live, both are only expressions of *one and the same* personal development of people and are therefore only in *seeming* contradiction to each other. As regards the position — determined by the special circumstances of development and by division of labour — which falls to the lot of the given individual, whether he represents to a greater extent one or the other aspect of the antithesis, whether he appears more as an egoist or more as selfless — that was a quite subordinate question, which could only acquire any interest at all if it were raised in definite epochs of history in relation to definite individuals. Otherwise this question could only lead to morally false, charlatan phrases. But as a dogmatist Sancho falls into error here and finds no other way out than by declaring that the Sancho Panzas and Don Quixotes are born such, and that then the Don Quixotes stuff all kinds of nonsense into the heads of the Sanchos; as a dogmatist he seizes on one aspect, conceived in a school-masterly manner, declares it to be characteristic of individuals as such, and expresses his aversion to the other aspect. Therefore, too, as a dogmatist, the other aspect appears to him partly as a mere *state of mind, dévoûment,* partly as a mere *"principle"*, and not as a relation necessarily arising from the preceding natural mode of life of individuals. One has, therefore, only to "get this principle out of one's head", although, according to Sancho's ideology, it creates all kinds of empirical things. Thus, for example: "social life, all sociability, all fraternity and all that... was created by the life principle or social principle." It is better the other way round: life created the principle.

Communism is quite incomprehensible to our saint because the communists do not oppose egoism to selflessness or selflessness to egoism, nor do they express this contradiction theoretically either in its sentimental or in its high-flown ideological form; they rather demonstrate its material source, with which it disappears of itself. The communists do not preach morality at all, as Stirner does so extensively. They do not put to people the moral demand: love one another, do not be egoists, etc.; on the contrary, they are very well aware that egoism, just as much as selflessness, is in definite circumstances a necessary form of the self-assertion of individuals.[123]

---

123 Cf. n. 102 above.

Hence, the communists by no means want, as Saint Max believes, to do away with the "private individual" for the sake of the "general", selfless man. That is a figment of the imagination concerning which one could already have found the necessary explanation in the *Deutsch-Französische Jahrbücher*. Communist theoreticians, the only communists who have time to devote to the study of history, are distinguished precisely by the fact that they alone have discovered that throughout history the "general interest" is created by individuals who are defined as "private persons". They know that this contradiction is only a seeming one because one side of it, what is called the "general interest", is constantly being produced by the other side, private interest, and in relation to the latter it is by no means an independent force with an independent history — so that this contradiction is in practice constantly destroyed and reproduced.[124] Hence it is not a question of the Hegelian "negative unity" of two sides of a contradiction, but of the materially determined destruction of the preceding materially determined mode of life of individuals, with the disappearance of which this contradiction together with its unity also disappears.

Thus we see how the "egoist in agreement with himself" as opposed to the "egoist in the ordinary sense" and the "selfless egoist", is based from the outset on an illusion about both of these and about the real relations of real people. The representative of personal interests is merely an "egoist in the ordinary sense" because of his necessary contradiction to communal interests which, within the existing mode of production and intercourse, are given

---

124 In other words, there is a coincidence — which Stirner misses — between egoism and class consciousness (this perhaps just to underscore a point I've already underlined numerous times in my annotations to this text).

an independent existence as general interests and are conceived and vindicated in the form of ideal interests. The representative of the interests of the community is merely "selfless" because of his opposition to personal interests, fixed as private interests, and because the interests of the community are defined as general and ideal interests. Both the "selfless egoist" and the "egoist in the ordinary sense" coincide, in the final analysis, in self-denial.

(ii)

> "No sheep, no dog, endeavours to become a real egoist. No animal calls to the others: 'Only know yourselves, only know what you are in reality.' — It is your nature to be egoistical, you are egoistical natures, i.e., egoists. But precisely because you are that already, you have no need to become so."

To what you are belongs also your consciousness, and since you are egoists you possess also the consciousness corresponding to your egoism, and therefore there is no reason at all for paying the slightest heed to Stirner's moral preaching to look into your heart and do penance.

Here again Stirner exploits an old philosophical device. The philosopher does not say directly: "You are not people." He says: "You have always been people, but you were not *conscious* of what you were, and for that very reason you were not in reality True People. Therefore your appearance was not appropriate to your essence. You were people and you were not people."

In a roundabout way the philosopher here admits that a definite consciousness is appropriate to definite people and definite circumstances. But at the same time he imagines that his moral demand to people — the demand that they should change their consciousness — will bring about this altered consciousness, and in people who have changed owing to changed empirical conditions and who, of course, now also possess a different consciousness, he sees nothing but a changed consciousness.

It is just the same with the consciousness for which you are secretly longing; in regard to this you are secret, unconscious egoists — i.e., you are really egoists, insofar as you are unconscious, but you are non-egoists, insofar as you are conscious. Or: at the root of your present consciousness lies a definite being, which is not the being which I demand; your consciousness is the consciousness of the egoist such as he should not be, and therefore it shows that you yourselves are egoists such as egoists should not be — or it shows that you should be different from what you really are. This entire separation of consciousness from the individuals who are its basis and from their actual conditions, this notion that the egoist of present-day bourgeois society does not possess the consciousness corresponding to his egoism, is merely an old philosophical fad that *Jacques le bonhomme* here credulously accepts and copies. Let us deal with Stirner's "touching example" of the avaricious person. He wants to persuade this avaricious person, who is not an "avaricious person" in general, but the avaricious "Tom or Dick"; a quite individually defined, "unique" avaricious person, whose avarice is not the category of "avarice" (an abstraction of Saint Max's from his all-embracing, complex, "unique" manifestation of life) and "does not depend on the heading under which other people" (for example, Saint Max) "classify it" — he wants to persuade this avaricious person by moral exhortations that he "is satisfying not himself but one of his desires". When Saint Max announces that I am satisfying only one of my desires, and not myself, he puts me as a complete and whole being in opposition to me myself.

"And in what does this complete and whole being consist? It is certainly not your momentary being, not what you are at the present moment."

Hence, according to Saint Max himself, it consists in the holy "being." When "Stirner" says that I must change my consciousness, then I know for my part that my momentary consciousness also belongs to my momentary being, and Saint Max, by disputing that I have this consciousness, attacks as a covert moralist my whole mode of life. And then: "do you exist only when you think about yourself, do you exist only owing to self-consciousness?"

How can I be anything but an egoist? How can Stirner, for example, be anything but an egoist — whether he denies egoism or not? "You are egoists and you are not egoists, inasmuch as you deny egoism" — that is what you preach.

Innocent, "deceived", "unavowed" school-master! Things are just the reverse. We egoists in the ordinary sense, we bourgeois, know quite well: "Charity begins at home", and we have long had the motto: love thy neighbour as thyself — interpreted in the sense that each is his own neighbour. But we deny that we are heartless egoists, exploiters, ordinary egoists, whose hearts cannot be lifted up to the exalted feeling of making the interests of their fellow-men their own — which, between ourselves, only means that we declare our interests to be the interests of our fellow-men. You deny the "ordinary" egoism of the unique egoist only because you "deny" your "natural relations to the world". Hence you do not understand why we bring practical egoism to perfection precisely by denying the phraseology of egoism — we who are concerned with realising real egoistical interests, not the *holy* interest of egoism.

Incidentally, it could be foreseen — and here the bourgeois coolly turns his back on Saint Max — that you German school-masters, if you once took up the defence of egoism, would proclaim not real, "mundane and plainly evident" egoism, that is to say, "not what is called" egoism, but egoism in the extraordinary, school-masterly sense, philosophical or vagabond egoism. The egoist in the extraordinary sense, therefore, is "only now discovered". "Let us examine this new discovery more closely."

From what has been just said it is already clear that the egoists who existed till now have only to change their consciousness in order to become egoists in the extraordinary sense, hence that the egoist in agreement with himself is distinguished from the previous type only by consciousness, i.e., only as a learned man, as a philosopher. It further follows from the whole historical outlook of Saint Max that, because the former egoists were ruled only by the "holy", the true egoist has to fight only against the "holy". "Unique" history has shown us how Saint Max transformed historical conditions into ideas, and then the egoist into a sinner against these ideas; how every egoistic manifestation was transformed into a sin against these ideas, the power of the privileged into a sin against the idea of equality, into the sin of despotism.

(iii)

Stirner's objections to communism were nothing but a preliminary, concealed legitimisation of his egoism in agreement with itself, in which these objections are resurrected in the flesh. The *"equal well-being of all in one and the same respect"* is resurrected in the demand that "we should only feel happy in dissolution." "Care" is resurrected to secure one's ego as one's property; but "with the passage of time" "care" again arises as to "how" one can arrive at a unity — viz., unity of creator and creation. And, finally, humanism re-appears, which in the form of the true egoist confronts empirical individuals as an unattainable ideal.

Egoism in agreement with itself really endeavours to transform every man into a "secret police state". The spy and sleuth "reflection" keeps a strict eye on every impulse of spirit and body, and every deed and thought, every manifestation of life is, for him, a matter of reflection, i.e. a police matter. It is this dismemberment of man into "natural instinct" and "reflection" (the inner plebeian — creation; and the internal police — creator) which constitutes the egoist in agreement with himself.[125]

Thus, the attitude of the true egoist as creator towards himself as creation was first of all defined in the sense that in opposition to a definition in which he became fixed as a creation — for example, as against himself as thinker, as spirit — he asserts himself as a person also-otherwise-determined, as flesh. Later, he no longer asserts himself as *really* also-otherwise-determined, but as the *mere idea*

---

125 One of the perennial problems of philosophy since Descartes concerns the artificial separation of "mind" from "world" — Cartesian Dualism, a doctrine which has been almost universally rejected, but which no philosopher ever seems able to completely overcome (see John McDowell's *Mind and World* for a relatively recent attempt to grapple with the problem). Here Marx and Engels identify this dualism — along with certain problems associated with it — in Stirner. In many ways their critique here follows from their discussion of another perennial artificial dualism — that between "nature" and "history", as discussed by me in n. 30 above. By maintaining a hard-and-fast distinction between "the ego" and "the flesh" — between mind, in short, and world — Stirner alienates the instincts from any sort of thinking about them. He turns us into creatures who are forever having to struggle to keep ourselves in check — troublesome flesh-puppets kept in check with absolute licence by some abstract force, steely and withdrawn.

of being also-otherwise-determined in general — hence, in the above example as someone who also-does-not-think, who is thoughtless or indifferent to thought, an idea which he abandons again as soon as its nonsensicalness becomes evident. See above on turning round on the heel of speculation. Hence the creative activity consisted here in the reflection that this single determination, in the present case thought, could also be indifferent for him, i.e., it consisted in reflecting in general; as a result, of course, he creates only reflective definitions, if he creates anything at all (e.g., the idea of antithesis, the simple essence of which is concealed by all kinds of fiery arabesques).

As for the *content* of himself as a creation, we have seen that nowhere does he create this content, these definite qualities, e.g., his thought, his zeal, etc., but only the reflective definition of this content as creation, the idea that these definite qualities are his creations. All his qualities are present in him and whence they come is all the same to him. He, therefore, needs neither to develop them — for example, to learn to dance, in order to have mastery over his feet, or to exercise his thought on material which is not given to everyone, and is not procurable by everyone, in order to become the owner of his thought — nor does he need to worry about the conditions in the world, which in reality determine the extent to which an individual can develop.

Stirner actually only rids himself of one quality by means of another (i.e., the suppression of his remaining qualities by this "other"). In reality, however, as we have already shown, he does this only insofar as this quality has not only achieved free development, i.e., has not remained merely potential, but also insofar as conditions in the world have permitted him to develop in an equal measure a *totality* of qualities, that is to say, thanks to the division of labour, thus making possible the predominant pursuit of a single passion, e.g., that of writing books. In general, it is an absurdity to assume, as Saint Max does, that one could satisfy one passion, apart from all others, that one could satisfy it without at the same time satisfying *oneself*, the entire living individual.[126] If this passion assumes an abstract, isolated character, if it confronts me as an alien power, if, therefore, the satisfaction of the individual appears as the one-sided satisfaction of a single passion — this by no means depends on consciousness or "good will" and least of all on lack of reflection on the concept of this quality, as Saint Max imagines.

It depends not on *consciousness*, but on *being*; not on thought, but on life; it depends on the individual's empirical development and manifestation of life, which in turn depends on the conditions obtaining in the world. If the circumstances in which the individual lives allow him only the one-sided development of one quality at the expense of all the rest, if they give him the material and time to develop only that one quality, then this individual achieves only a one-sided, crippled development. No moral preaching avails here. And the manner in which this one, pre-eminently favoured quality develops depends again, on the one hand, on the material available for its development and, on the other hand, on the degree and manner in which the other qualities are suppressed. Precisely because thought, for example, is the thought of a particular, definite individual, it remains his definite thought, determined by his individuality and the conditions in which he lives. The thinking individual therefore has no need to resort to prolonged reflection about thought as such in order to declare that his thought is his own thought, his property; from the outset it is his own, peculiarly determined thought

---

126 Compare the stuff about hunting and fishing and critically criticising in Chapter 1 above.

and it was precisely his peculiarity which in the case of Saint Sancho was found to be the "opposite" of this, a peculiarity which is peculiarity "*as such*". In the case of an individual, for example, whose life embraces a wide circle of varied activities and practical relations to the world, and who, therefore, lives a many-sided life, thought has the same character of universality as every other manifestation of his life. Consequently, it neither becomes fixed in the form of abstract thought nor does it need complicated tricks of reflection when the individual passes from thought to some other manifestation of life. From the outset it is always a factor in the total life of the individual, one which disappears and is reproduced as required.

In the case of a parochial Berlin school-master or author, however, whose activity is restricted to arduous work on the one hand and the pleasure of thought on the other, whose world extends from Moabit to Köpenick and ends behind the Hamburger Tor,[127] whose relations to this world are reduced to a minimum by his pitiful position in life, when such an individual experiences the need to think, it is indeed inevitable that his thought becomes just as abstract as he himself and his life, and that thought confronts him, who is quite incapable of resistance, in the form of a fixed power, whose activity offers the individual the possibility of a momentary escape from his "bad world", of a momentary pleasure. In the case of such an individual the few remaining desires, which arise not so much from intercourse with the world as from the constitution of the human body, express themselves only through *repercussion*, i.e., they assume in their narrow development the same one-sided and crude character as does his thought, they appear only at long intervals, stimulated by the excessive

---

127 These are all places in Berlin. Stirner's life as Marx describes it would be considerably more aspirational nowadays.

development of the predominant desire (fortified by immediate physical causes, e.g., stomach spasms) and are manifested turbulently and forcibly, with the most brutal suppression of the ordinary, natural desire — this leads to further domination over thought. As a matter of course, the school-master's thinking reflects on and speculates about this empirical fact in a school- masterly fashion. But the mere announcement that Stirner in general "creates" his qualities does not explain even their particular form of development. The extent to which these qualities develop on the universal or local scale, the extent to which they transcend local narrow-mindedness or remain within its confines, depends not on Stirner, but on the development of world intercourse and on the part which he and the locality where he lives play in it. That under favourable circumstances some individuals are able to rid themselves of their local narrow-mindedness is by no means due to individuals imagining that they have got rid of, or intend to get rid of their local narrow-mindedness, but is only due to the fact that in their real empirical life individuals, actuated by empirical needs, have been able to bring about world intercourse.

The only thing our saint achieves with the aid of his arduous reflection about his qualities and passions is that by his constant crotchetiness and scuffling with them he poisons the enjoyment and satisfaction of them.

Saint Max creates, as already said, only himself as a creation, i.e., he is satisfied with placing himself in this category of created entity. His activity as creator consists in regarding himself as a creation, and he does not even go on to resolve this division of himself into creator and creation, which is his own product. The division into the "essential" and the "inessential" becomes for him a permanent life process, hence mere appearance, i.e., his real life exists only in "pure" reflection, is not even actual existence; for since this latter is at every instant outside him and his reflection, he tries in vain to present reflection as essential.

Stirner is a "posited man", since he is always a posited ego, and his ego is "also a man." "For that reason" he is a posited man; "for since" he is never driven by his passions to excesses, "therefore", he is what burghers call a sedate man, "*but*" the fact that he is a sedate man "signifies merely" that he always keeps an account of his own transformations and refractions.

(iv)

> "Do not seek in 'self-denial' the freedom that actually deprives you of yourselves, but seek yourselves, become egoists, each of you should become an all-powerful ego!"

After the foregoing, we should not be surprised if later on Saint Max's attitude to this proposition is again that of creator and most irreconcilable enemy and he "dissolves" his lofty moral postulate: "Become an *all-powerful* ego" into this, that each, in any case, does what he can, and that he can do what he does, and therefore, of course, for Saint Max, he is "*all-powerful*".

Incidentally, the nonsense of the egoist in agreement with himself is summarised in the proposition quoted above. First comes the moral injunction to seek and, moreover, to seek oneself. This is defined in the sense that man should become something that he so far is not, namely, an egoist, and this egoist is defined as being an "all-powerful ego," in whom the peculiar ability has become resolved from actual ability into the ego, into omnipotence, into the fantastic idea of ability. To seek oneself means, therefore, to become something different from what one is and, indeed, to become *all-powerful,* i.e., *nothing*, a non-thing, a phantasmagoria.

The Revelation of John the Divine, or: "The Logic of the New Wisdom"[128]

(i)

I am not the people.
> The people = non-I
> I = the non-people.

Hence, I am the negation of the people, the people is dissolved in me. The people's ego is non-existent — the ego of the people is the negation of my ego.[129]

(ii)

We have already seen above how Saint Sancho separates the ideas of individuals from the conditions of their life, from their practical collisions and contradictions, in order then to transform them into the holy. Now these ideas appear in the form of *designation, vocation, task*. For Saint Sancho vocation has a double form; firstly as the vocation which others choose for me — examples of which we have already had above in the case of the newspapers that are

---

128 I'm not sure why Marx and Engels decided to name this section after the Apocalypse.

129 This, of course, is Marx and Engels's gloss of Stirner's view. With the implication being: well, of course, this is absurd. Yes, if we conjure up some spook called "the people", then it will turn out that none of us is *quite* a member of it. But that's not *actually* what we ought to be thinking about, when we start to theorise or plot or strategise or whatever in supra-individualistic terms. What is important is things like, "the workers at the factory"; "the class" — collectives with which *of course* it might make sense to identify me, as an individual, as a member.

full of politics and the prisons that our saint mistook for houses of moral correction. Afterwards vocation appears also as a vocation in which the individual himself believes. If the ego is divorced from all its empirical conditions of life, its activity, the conditions of its existence, if it is separated from the world that forms its basis and from its own body, then, of course, it has no other vocation and no other designation than that of representing the Caius of the logical proposition[130] and to assist Saint Sancho in arriving at the equations given above. In the real world, on the other hand, where individuals have needs, they thereby already have a vocation and task; and at the outset it is still immaterial whether they make this their vocation in their imagination as well. It is clear, however, that because the individuals possess consciousness they form an idea of this vocation which their empirical existence has given them and, thus, furnish Saint Sancho with the opportunity of seizing on the word vocation, that is, on the mental expression of their actual conditions of life, and of leaving out of account these conditions of life themselves.

The proletarian, for example, who like every human being has the vocation of satisfying his needs and who is not in a position to satisfy even the needs that he has in common with all human beings, the proletarian whom the necessity to work a 14-hour day debases to the level of

---

130 This line took me literal years to figure out. Reading it, I was just like: "yeah, but who the fuck is *Caius?*" What could this possibly be a reference to? Caligula (that is, Gaius Caesar)? King Lear? (Kent appears disguised as "Caius"). Anyway, it turns out that in German logic textbooks of the time, "Caius" was the stock figure you'd use in syllogisms, as we typically use "Socrates" nowadays: "Caius is a man, all men are mortal, etc.". So it's pretty straightforward really.

a beast of burden, whom competition degrades to a mere thing, an article of trade, who from his position as a mere productive force, the sole position left to him, is squeezed out by other, more powerful productive forces — this proletarian is, if only for these reasons, confronted with the real task of revolutionising his conditions. He can, of course, imagine this to be his "vocation", he can also, if he likes to engage in propaganda, express his "vocation" by saying that to do this or that is the human vocation of the proletarian, the more so since his position does not even allow him to satisfy the needs arising directly from his human nature. Saint Sancho does not concern himself with the reality underlying this idea, with the practical aim of this proletarian — he clings to the word "vocation" and declares it to be the holy, and the proletarian to be a servant of the holy — the easiest way of considering himself superior and "proceeding further".

Particularly in the relations that have existed hitherto, when one class always ruled, when the conditions of life of an individual always coincided with the conditions of life of a class, when, therefore, the practical task of each newly emerging class was bound to appear to each of its members as a universal task, and when each class could actually overthrow its predecessor only by liberating the individuals of all classes from certain chains which had hitherto fettered them — under these circumstances it was essential that the task of the individual members of a class striving for domination should be described as a universal human task.

Incidentally, when for example the bourgeois tells the proletarian that his, the proletarian's, human task is to work fourteen hours a day, the proletarian is quite justified in replying in the same language that on the contrary his task is to overthrow the entire bourgeois system.

(iii)

Just as Saint Sancho canonises communism in order later, in connection with the union,[131] the better to palm off his holy idea of it as his "own" invention, so, in exactly the same way, he blusters against "vocation, designation, task" merely in order to reproduce them throughout his book as the *categorical imperative*. Wherever difficulties arise, Sancho hacks his way through them by means of a categorical imperative such as "turn yourself to account", "recognise yourself", "let each become an all-powerful ego", etc.

(iv)

When Saint Sancho is starving to death it is not due to lack of food, but to his own hungriness, his own quality of starving. If he falls out of a window and breaks his neck, it happens not because the force of gravity plunges him downwards, but because absence of wings, inability to fly, is a quality of his own.[132]

---

131 Stirner's ideal society would be a "union of egoists", in which ideally egoistic individuals exist somehow together, but are in no way bound by one another (they don't even have any sort of conventional respect for one another's property rights). Marx and Engels spend quite a bit of the "Sankt Max" manuscript explaining what is wrong with this idea. I haven't included any of the text, however, as it is too long-winded to be genuinely illuminating. Basically, the take-home message is: Stirner thinks his "union of egoists" is radically different from bourgeois society, but actually (according to Marx and Engels) all he really manages to achieve is to *describe* it.

132 An inversion of the joke Marx and Engels tell in the Preface about a philosopher who spent his whole life raging against the "idea" of gravity.

Solomon's Song of Songs, or: The Unique[133]

Cease man of Troy, and cease thou sage of Greece,
To boast of Navigations great ye made;
Let the high Fame of Alexander cease,
And Trajan's Banners in the East display'd:
Cease All, whose Actions ancient Bards exprest:
A brighter Valour arises in the West.
And you my Spree Nymphs...
Give me a mighty Fury, Nor rude Reeds
Or rustic Bag-Pipes sound, But such as War's
Lowd Instrument (the noble Trumpet) breeds,
Which fires the Breast, and stirs the blood to jars.[134]

Give me, o nymphs of the Spree, a song worthy of the heroes who
fight on your banks against Substance and Man,
a song that will spread over the whole world and will be sung in all lands —
for it is a matter here of the man whose deeds are

---

133 Obviously a reference to the Song of Songs from the Bible, which occupies a unique place within the Old Testament — an ecstatic celebration of sexual love. In the Christian tradition, the Song has typically been read as an allegory of the love of Christ for the Church (bit weird, but there you go). Presumably, here the joke is that Stirner's book is really just the celebration of the love he — Stirner — has for himself.

134 All italicised lines here are from Luís de Camões's epic *The Luisiads* (with some slight alterations by Marx and Engels, for instance by swapping out references to the Tagus for the Spree), and are in Portugal in the original. First published in 1572, the poem is a Homeric celebration of the achievements of the Portuguese Age of Discovery.

Beyond what strength of human nature here.

Greater than mere "human" power can perform,
The man who

acquir'd
A modern Scepter which to Heaven aspired.

Who has founded a new kingdom among a far-off people,
viz. the 'union' –
it is a matter of here being a

– fair and tender Blossom of that Tree
Belov'd by Him, Who dy'd on one for Man.

Of the tender and young blossoming shoot of a tree
especially loved by Christ,
a tree which is nothing less than

certain hope t'extend the Pale,
One day, of narrow Christianitie,

the surest hope of growth for faint-hearted Christianity –
in a word, it is a matter of something "unprecendented",
the "unique".

Everything that is to be found in this unprecedented song
of songs about the unique was in existence earlier in the
"book". We mention this chapter only for the sake of good
order; so that we should be able to do it properly we have
left the examination of some points until now and we shall
briefly recapitulate others.

Sancho's "ego" has gone through the full gamut of soul
migration. We already met it as the egoist in agreement
with himself, as *corvée* peasant, as trader in thoughts, as

unfortunate competitor, as owner, as a slave who has had one of his legs torn out, as Sancho tossed into the air by the interaction between birth and circumstances, and in a hundred other shapes. Here it bids us farewell as an *"inhuman being"*, under the same banner as that under which it made its entry into the New Testament.

"Only the *inhuman being* is the *real* man."

This is one of the thousand and one equations in which Sancho expounds his legend of the holy.

The concept "man" is not the real man.

The concept "man" = Man.
Man = not the real man.
The real man = the non-man
          = the inhuman being.

"Only the inhuman being is the real man."

Sancho tries to explain to himself the harmlessness of this proposition by means of the following transformations:

"It is not so difficult to express in a few plain words what an inhuman being is; it is a man... who does not correspond to the concept of what is human. Logic calls this a nonsensical judgment. Would one have the right to pronounce this judgment that someone can be a man without being a man, if one did not admit the validity of the hypothesis that the concept of man can be separated from his existence, that the essence can be separated from the appearance? People say: so and so seems to be a man, but he is not a man. People have pronounced this nonsensical judgment throughout many centuries: moreover, during this long period of time there have only been inhuman beings. What individual did ever correspond to his concept?"

This passage is again based on our school-master's fantasy about the school-master who has created for himself an ideal of "Man" and "put it into the heads" of other people, a fantasy which forms the basic theme of "the book".

Sancho calls it a hypothesis that the concept and existence, the essence and appearance of "man" can be separated, as though the possibility of this separation is not already expressed in the very words he uses. When he says *concept*, he is speaking of something different from *existence*; when he says *essence*, he is speaking of something different from *appearance*. It is not these *statements* that he brings into contradiction, but they themselves are the expressions of a contradiction. Hence the only question that could have been raised is whether it is permissible for him to range something under these points of view; and in order to deal with this Sancho would have had to consider the actual relations of people who have been given other names in these metaphysical relations. For the rest, Sancho's own arguments about the egoist in agreement with himself and about rebellion show how these points of view can be made to diverge, while his arguments about peculiarity, possibility and reality — in connection with "self-enjoyment" — show how they can be made simultaneously to coincide and to diverge.

The nonsensical judgment of the philosophers that the real man is not man is in the sphere of abstraction merely the most universal, all-embracing expression of the actually existing universal contradiction between the conditions and needs of people. The nonsensical form of the abstract proposition fully corresponds to the nonsensical character, carried to extreme lengths, of the relations of bourgeois society, just as Sancho's nonsensical judgment about his environment — they are egoists and at the same time they are not egoists — corresponds to the actual contradiction between the existence of the German petty bourgeois and the tasks which existing relations have imposed on them and which they themselves entertain in the form of pious wishes and desires. Incidentally, philosophers have declared people to be inhuman, not because they did not correspond to the concept of man, but because their concept of man did not correspond to the true concept of man, or because they had no true understanding of man. *Tout comme chez nous*,[135] in "the book", where Sancho also declares that people are non-egoists for the sole reason that they have no true understanding of egoism.

In view of its extreme triviality and indisputable certainty, there should have been no need to mention the perfectly inoffensive proposition that the *idea* of man is not the *real* man, that the idea of a thing is not the thing itself — a proposition which is also applicable to a stone and to the idea of a stone, in accordance with which Sancho should have said that the real stone is non-stone. But Sancho's well-known fantasy that only because of the domination of ideas and concepts mankind has up to now been subjected to all sorts of misfortunes, makes it possible for him to link his old conclusions again with this proposition. Sancho's old opinion that one has only to get a few ideas out of one's head in order to abolish from the world the conditions which have given rise to these ideas, is reproduced here in the form that one has only to get out of one's *head* the idea of man in order to put an end to the actually existing conditions which are today called inhuman — whether this predicate "inhuman" expresses

---

135 "Just as with us" — apparently, this is a reference to a play in which the stock character Harlequin is making up things about life on the Moon.

the opinion of the individual in contradiction with his conditions or the opinion of the normal, ruling society about the abnormal, subjected class. In just the same way, a whale taken from the ocean and put in the *Kupfergraben*,[136] if it possessed consciousness, would declare this situation created by "unfavourable circumstances" to be unwhale-like, although Sancho could prove that it is whale-like, if only because it is its, the whale's, own situation — that is precisely how people argue in certain circumstances.

At one point, Sancho raises the important question:

> "But how to curb the inhuman being who dwells in each individual? How can one manage not to set free the inhuman being along with the human being? All liberalism has a mortal enemy, an invincible opponent, as God has the devil; at the side of the human being there is always the inhuman being, the egoist, the individual. State, society, mankind cannot master this devil."

In the form in which Sancho understands it, the question again becomes sheer nonsense. He imagines that people up to now have always formed a concept of man, and then won freedom for themselves to the extent that was necessary to realise this concept; that the measure of freedom that they achieved was determined each time by their idea of the ideal of man at the time; it was thus unavoidable that in each individual there remained a residue which did not correspond to this ideal and, hence, since it was "inhuman", was either not set free or only freed *malgré eux*.[137]

In reality, of course, what happened was that people won freedom for themselves each time to the extent that was dictated and permitted not by their ideal of man, but

---

136 A section of the Spree in the middle of Berlin.
137 "Despite them."

by the existing productive forces. All emancipation carried through hitherto has been based, however, on restricted productive forces. The production which these productive forces could provide was insufficient for the whole of society and made development possible only if some persons satisfied their needs at the expense of others, and therefore some — the minority — obtained the monopoly of development, while others — the majority — owing to the constant struggle to satisfy their most essential needs, were for the time being (i.e., until the creation of new revolutionary productive forces) excluded from any development. Thus, society has hitherto always developed within the framework of a contradiction — in antiquity the contradiction between free men and slaves, in the Middle Ages that between nobility and serfs, in modern times that between the bourgeoisie and the proletariat. This explains, on the one hand, the abnormal, "inhuman" way in which the oppressed class satisfies its needs, and, on the other hand, the narrow limits within which intercourse, and with it the whole ruling class, develops. Hence this restricted character of development consists not only in the exclusion of one class from development, but also in the narrow-mindedness of the excluding class, and the "inhuman" is to be found also within the ruling class. This so-called "inhuman" is just as much a product of present-day relations as the "human" is; it is their negative aspect, the rebellion — which is not based on any new revolutionary productive force — against the prevailing relations brought about by the existing productive forces, and against the way of satisfying needs that corresponds to these relations. The positive expression "human" corresponds to the definite relations *predominant* at a certain stage of production and to the way of satisfying needs determined by them, just as the negative expression "inhuman" corresponds to the attempt to negate these predominant relations and the way of satisfying needs prevailing under them without changing the existing mode of production, an attempt that this stage of production daily engenders afresh.

For our saint, such world-historical struggles are reduced to a mere collision between Saint Bruno and "the mass". Thus, our simple-minded Sancho with his naive little statement about the inhuman being and with his talk of getting-man-out-of-one's-head, thanks to which the inhuman being also disappears and there is no longer any measure for individuals, finally arrives at the following result. He regards the physical, intellectual and social crippling and enslavement which as a result of the existing relations afflict an individual, as the individuality and peculiarity of that individual; like an ordinary conservative he calmly recognises these relations once he has freed his mind of all worry by getting out of his head the philosophers' idea of these relations. Just as here he declares fortuitous features imposed on the individual to be the latter's individuality, so earlier, in connection with the ego, he abstracted not only from any fortuity, but also in general from any individuality.

About the "inhuman" great result obtained by him Sancho sings in the following *Kyrie eleison*,[138] which he puts into the mouth of "the inhuman being":

"*I was despicable because I sought my better self outside me;*
I was the inhuman, because I dreamed of the human;
I was like the pious ones who hunger for their true ego and always remain poor
sinners;
I thought of myself only in comparison with someone else;
I was not all in all, I was not — unique.

---

138 Christian prayer often set to music — literal translation "Lord, have mercy".

Now, however, I cease to appear to myself as the inhuman;
I cease to measure myself by man and to let others measure me;
I cease to recognise anything above myself —
I was inhuman, but I am no longer inhuman, I am the unique!"
Hallelujah!

We shall not dwell further here on how "the inhuman" —
which, it may be said in passing, put itself in the right frame
of mind by *"turning its back"* "on *itself* and the critic", Saint
Bruno — how "the inhuman" here *"appears"*, or does not
"appear" to *itself*. We shall only point out that the "unique"
(it or he) is characterised here by his getting the holy out
of his head for the nine-hundredth time, whereby, as we in
our turn are compelled to repeat for the nine-hundredth
time, everything remains as before, not to mention the fact
that it is no more than a pious wish.

We have here, for the first time, the unique person,
Sancho, who with the litany mentioned above has received
the accolade of knighthood, now appropriates his new,
noble name. Sancho arrives at his uniqueness by getting
"Man" out of his head. He thereby ceases "to think of himself
only in comparison with someone else" and "to recognise
something above him." He becomes incomparable. This is
again the same old fantasy of Sancho's that it is not the
needs of individuals, but concepts, ideas, "the holy" —
here in the shape of "Man" — that are the sole *tertium
comparationis*[139] and the sole bond between individuals.
Sancho, who notices nothing but "the holy", need not
bother about the fact that it is through their needs that
individuals are linked together, and that the development
of the productive forces up to now implies the domination

---

139 "The third part of the comparison" — the quality that two
things that are being compared have in common.

of one section over the other. He gets an idea out of his head and thereby becomes unique.

To become "unique" in his sense of the word he must above all prove to us his *freedom from premises*.

> "Your thought has as its premise not thought, but you. But thus you nevertheless have yourself as a premise? Yes, but not to me, but to my thought. I am before my thought. It follows hence that no thought precedes my thinking, or that my thinking is without any premise. For the premise which I am for my thinking is not one created by thinking, not one that is thought, but... is the owner of thinking, and proves only that thinking is nothing but — property."

"We are prepared to allow" that Sancho does not think before he thinks, and that he and everyone else is in this respect a thinker without premises. Similarly we concede that he does not have any thought as the premise of his existence, i.e., that he was not created by thoughts. If for a moment Sancho abstracts from all his thoughts — which with his meagre assortment cannot be very difficult[140] — there remains his real ego, but his real ego within the framework of the actual relations of the world that exist for it. In this way he has divested himself for a moment of all dogmatic premises, but now for the first time the *real* premises begin to come to light for him. And these real premises are also the premises of his *dogmatic* premises which, whether he likes it or not, will reappear to him together with the real ones so long as he does not obtain different real premises, and with them also different dogmatic premises, or so long as he does not recognise in a materialistic way that the real premises are the premises of his thinking, and as

---

140 Alright, lads — you're the ones who wrote like hundreds of thousands of words exhaustively critiquing the guy.

a result his dogmatic ones will disappear altogether. Just as his development up to now and his Berlin environment have at present led to the dogmatic premise of egoism in agreement with itself, so, despite all imaginary freedom from premises, this premise will remain with him as long as he fails to overcome its real premises.

As a true school-master, Sancho still continues to strive for the famous Hegelian "premiseless thinking", i.e., thinking without dogmatic premises, which in Hegel too is only a pious wish.[141] Sancho believed he could achieve this by a skilful leap and even surpass it by going in pursuit of the premiseless ego. But both the one and the other eluded his grasp.

Then Sancho tries his luck in another fashion:

> "Make full use of the demand for freedom! Who shall become free? You, I, we. Free from what? From everything that is not you, not I, not we. I, therefore, am the core... What remains if I become free from everything that is not I? Only I and nothing but I."

"Everything that is not you, not I, not we" is, of course, here again a dogmatic idea, like state, nationality, division of labour, etc. Once these ideas have been subjected to criticism — and, in Sancho's opinion, this has already been done by "criticism", namely critical criticism — he again imagines that he is also free from the actual state, actual nationality and division of labour. Consequently the ego, which is here the "core," which "has become free from everything that is not I" — is still the above-mentioned premiseless ego with everything that it has not got rid of.

If, however, Sancho were once to tackle the subject of "becoming free" with the desire of freeing himself not

---

141 See n. 16 above.

merely from categories, but from actual fetters, then such liberation would presuppose a change common to him and to a large mass of other people, and would produce a change in the state of the world which again would be common to him and others. Although his "ego" "remains" after liberation, it is hereafter a totally changed ego sharing with others a changed state of the world which is precisely the premise, common to him and others, of his and their freedom, and it follows that the uniqueness, incomparability and independence of his "ego" again come to nothing.

Sancho tries again in a third fashion:

"Their disgrace is not that [Jew and Christian] *exclude* each other but that this only *half* occurs. If they could be perfect egoists they would *totally* exclude each other."

"If one desires *only to resolve* the contradiction one grasps its meaning in too formal and feeble a way. The contradiction deserves rather to be sharpened."

"Only when you recognise your contradiction fully and when everyone asserts himself from head to foot as *unique* will you no longer simply conceal your contradiction... The final and most decisive contradiction — that between one unique person and another — goes basically beyond the bounds of what is called contradiction... As a unique person you have nothing more in common with the other and, for that reason, nothing that makes you separate from him or hostile to him... Contradiction disappears in perfect... separateness or uniqueness."

"I do not *want* to have or to be something special in relation to others; nor do I measure myself by others... I want to be everything I can be, and to have everything I can have.

What do I care whether others are or have *something similar* to me? They can neither be nor have something equal, the same. I do nothing detrimental to them any more than it is to the detriment of the cliff that I have the advantage of movement. If they could have it, they would have it. Doing nothing to the detriment of other people, that is the meaning of the demand to have no privilege... One should not regard oneself as 'something *special*', e.g., Jew or Christian. Well, I regard myself not as something special but as *unique*. True, I have a resemblance to others; but this holds only for comparison or reflection; in fact, however, I am incomparable, unique. My flesh is not their flesh, my spirit is not their spirit. If you bring them under the *general concept* 'flesh', 'spirit', then those are your thoughts, which have nothing to do with my flesh, my spirit."

"Human society perishes because of the egoists, for they no longer treat one another as human beings, but act egoistically as an ego against a you that is totally distinct from and hostile to me."

"As though one individual will not always seek out another, and as though one person does not have to adapt himself to another, when he needs him. But the difference is that in this case the individual actually unites with another individual, whereas previously he was linked to him by a bond."

"Only when you are unique can you in your intercourse with one another be what you actually are."

The bombastic phrases about "contradiction" which has to be sharpened and taken to extremes, and about the "something special", which Sancho does not want to have as his advantage, amount to one and the same thing.

Sancho wants, or rather *believes* he wants, that intercourse between individuals should be purely personal, that their intercourse should not be mediated through some third thing. This third thing here is the "something special", or the special — not absolute — contradiction, i.e., the position of individuals in relation to one another determined by present-day social relations. Sancho does not want, for example, two individuals to be in "contradiction" to one another as bourgeois and proletarian; he protests against the "special" which forms the "advantage" of the bourgeois over the proletarian; he would like to have them enter into a purely personal relation, to associate with one another merely as individuals. He does not take into consideration that in the framework of division of labour personal relations necessarily and inevitably develop into class relations and become fixed as such and that, therefore, all his talk amounts simply to a pious wish, which he expects to realise by exhorting the individuals of these classes to get out of their heads the idea of their "contradiction" and their "special" "privilege". In the passages from Sancho quoted above, everything turns only on people's *opinion of themselves*, and *his* opinion of them, what they want and what he wants. "Contradiction" and the "special" are abolished by a change of "*opinion*" and "*wanting*".

Even that which constitutes the advantage of an individual as such over other individuals, is in our day at the same time a product of society and in its realisation is bound to assert itself as privilege, as we have already shown Sancho in connection with competition. Further, the individual as such, regarded by himself, is subordinated to division of labour, which makes him one-sided, cripples and determines him.

What, at best, does Sancho's sharpening of contradiction and abolition of the special amount to? To this, that the mutual relations of individuals should be their behaviour to one another, while their mutual differences should be their *self-distinctions* (as one empirical self distinguishes *itself* from another). Both of these are either, as with Sancho, an ideological paraphrase of *what exists*, for the relations of individuals under all circumstances can only be their mutual behaviour, while their differences can only be their self-distinctions. Or they are the pious wish that they *should* behave in *such a way* and differ from one another *in such a way*, that their behaviour does not acquire independent existence as a social relationship independent of them, and that their differences from one another should not assume the material character (independent of the person) which they have assumed and daily continue to assume.

Individuals have always and in all circumstances "proceeded *from themselves*", but since they were not *unique* in the sense of not needing any connections with one another, and since their needs, consequently their nature, and the method of satisfying their needs, connected them with one another (relations between the sexes, exchange, division of labour), they *had to* enter into relations with one another. Moreover, since they entered into intercourse with one another not as pure egos, but as individuals at a definite stage of development of their productive forces and requirements, and since this intercourse, in its turn, determined production and needs, it was, therefore, precisely the personal, individual behaviour of individuals, their behaviour to one another as individuals, that created the existing relations and daily reproduces them anew. They entered into intercourse with one another as what they were, they proceeded "from themselves", as they were, irrespective of their "outlook on life". This "outlook on life" — even the warped one of the philosophers — could, of course, only be determined by their actual life. Hence it certainly follows that the development of an individual is determined by the development of all the others with whom he is directly or indirectly associated, and that the different generations of individuals entering into relation with one another are connected with one another, that the physical existence of the later generations is determined by that of their predecessors, and that these later generations inherit the productive forces and forms of intercourse accumulated by their predecessors, their own mutual relations being determined thereby. In short, it is clear that development takes place and that the history of a single individual cannot possibly be separated from the history of preceding or contemporary individuals, but is determined by this history.

The transformation of the individual relationship into its opposite, a purely material relationship, the distinction of individuality and fortuity by the individuals themselves, is a historical process, as we have already shown, and at different stages of development it assumes different, ever sharper and more universal forms. In the present epoch, the domination of material relations over individuals, and the suppression of individuality by fortuitous circumstances, has assumed its sharpest and most universal form, thereby setting existing individuals a very definite task. It has set them the task of replacing the domination of circumstances and of chance over individuals by the domination of individuals over chance and circumstances. It has not, as Sancho imagines, put forward the demand that "I should develop myself", which up to now every individual has done without Sancho's good advice; it has on the contrary called for liberation from a quite definite mode of development. This task, dictated by present-day relations, coincides with the task of organising society in a communist way.

We have already shown above that the abolition of a state of affairs in which relations become independent of individuals, in which individuality is subservient to chance and the personal relations of individuals are subordinated to general class relations, etc. — that the abolition of this state of affairs is determined in the final analysis by the abolition of division of labour. We have also shown that the abolition of division of labour is determined by the development of intercourse and productive forces to such a degree of universality that private property and division of labour become fetters on them. We have further shown that private property can be abolished only on condition of an all-round development of individuals, precisely because the existing form of intercourse and the existing productive forces are all-embracing and only individuals that are developing in an all-round fashion can appropriate them, i.e., can turn them into free manifestations of their lives. We have shown that at the present time individuals *must* abolish private property, because the productive forces and forms of intercourse have developed so far that, under the domination of private property, they have become destructive forces, and because the contradiction between the classes has reached its extreme limit. Finally, we have shown that the abolition of private property and of the division of labour is itself the association of individuals on the basis created by modern productive forces and world intercourse.

Within communist society, the only society in which the genuine and free development of individuals ceases to be a mere phrase, this development is determined precisely by the connection of individuals, a connection which consists partly in the economic prerequisites and partly in the necessary solidarity of the free development of all, and, finally, in the universal character of the activity of individuals on the basis of the existing productive forces. We are, therefore, here concerned with individuals at a definite historical stage of development and by no means merely with individuals chosen at random, even disregarding the indispensable communist revolution, which itself is a general condition for their free development. The individuals' consciousness of their mutual relations will, of course, likewise be completely changed, and, therefore, will no more be the "principle of love" or *dévoûment* than it will be egoism.[142]

Thus, "uniqueness" — taken in the sense of genuine development and individual behaviour, as outlined above — presupposes not only things quite different from good will and right consciousness, but even the direct opposite of Sancho's fantasies. With him "uniqueness" is nothing more than an embellishment of existing conditions, a little drop of comforting balm for the poor, impotent soul that has become wretched through wretchedness.

As regards Sancho's *"incomparability"*, the situation is the same as with his "uniqueness". He himself will recall, if he is not completely "lost" in "sweet self-oblivion", that the organisation of labour in Stirner's "union of egoists" was based not only on the comparability of needs, but also on their *equality*. And he assumed not only equal needs, but also equal activity, so that one individual could take the place of another in "human work". And the extra remuneration of the "unique" person, crowning his efforts — what other basis had it than the fact that his performance was compared with that of others and in view of its superiority was better paid? And how can Sancho

---

142 Here we bear witness to a certain progression from Marx and Engels's previous comments about the coincidence between egoism and class consciousness. The revolution, if it happens, will happen out of egoism, not selflessness. But just as the victory of the proletariat over the bourgeoisie will result in the proletariat abolishing itself, so too will it abolish the egoistic self-interest that presently drives people. Communism is the overcoming of all existing conditions — egoism, "true" or otherwise — is just one more thing for it to overcome.

talk at all about incomparability when he allows *money* — the means of comparison that acquires independent existence in practice — to continue in being, subordinates himself to it and allows himself to be measured by this universal scale in order to be compared with others? It is quite evident that he himself gives the lie to his doctrine of incomparability. Nothing is easier than to call equality and inequality, similarity and dissimilarity, determinations of reflection. Incomparability too is a determination of reflection which has the activity of comparison as its premise. To show that comparison is not at all a purely arbitrary determination of reflection, it is enough to give just one example, *money*, the permanent *tertium comparationis* of all people and things.

Incidentally, incomparability can have different meanings. The only meaning in question here, namely "uniqueness" in the sense of originality, presupposes that the activity of the incomparable individual in a definite sphere differs from the activity of his *equals*. Persiani[143] is an incomparable singer precisely because she is a *singer* and is compared with other singers, and indeed by people who are able to recognise her incomparability through comparison based on normal hearing and musical training. Persiani's singing and the croaking of a frog are incomparable, although even here there could be a comparison, but it would be a comparison between a human being and a frog, and not between Persiani and a particular unique frog. Only in the first case is it possible to speak of a comparison between individuals, in the second it is a matter only of their properties as species or genus. A third type of incomparability — the incomparability of Persiani's singing with the tail of a comet — we leave to

---

143 Fanny Tacchinardi Persiani (1812-1867), Italian soprano singer.

Sancho for his "self-enjoyment", since at any rate he finds pleasure in "nonsensical judgments", although even this absurd comparison has a real basis in the absurdity of present-day relations. Money is the common measure for all, even the most heterogeneous things.

Incidentally, Sancho's incomparability amounts to the same empty phrase as his uniqueness. Individuals are no longer to be measured by some *tertium comparationis* independent of them, but comparison *should* be transformed into their self-distinction, i.e., into the free development of their individuality, which, moreover, is brought about by their getting "fixed ideas" out of their heads.

Incidentally, Sancho is acquainted only with the type of comparison made by scribblers and ranters, which leads to the magnificent conclusion that Sancho is not Bruno and Bruno is not Sancho. On the other hand, he is, of course, unacquainted with the sciences which have made considerable advances just by comparing and establishing differences in the spheres of comparison and in which comparison acquires a character of universal importance — i.e., in comparative anatomy, botany, philology, etc.

Great nations — the French, North Americans, English — are constantly comparing themselves with one another both in practice and theory, in competition and in science. Petty shopkeepers and philistines, like the Germans, who are afraid of comparison and competition, hide behind the shield of incomparability supplied them by their manufacturer of philosophical labels. Not only in their interests, but also in his own, has Sancho refused to tolerate any comparison.

The uniqueness, the originality, the "peculiar" development of individuals which, according to Sancho, does not for example occur in all "human works", although no one will deny that one stove-setter does not set a stove in the "*same*" way as another; the "unique" development of individuals which, in the opinion of this same Sancho, does not occur in religious, political, etc., spheres, although no one will deny that of all those who believe in Islam not one believes in it in the "same" way as another and to this extent each of them is "unique", just as among citizens not one has the "same" attitude to the state as another if only because it is a matter of his attitude, and not that of some *other* — all this much praised "uniqueness" which (according to Sancho) was so distinct from *"sameness", identity of the person*, that in all individuals who have so far existed he could hardly see anything but "specimens" of a species, is thus reduced here to the identity of a person with himself, as established by the police, to the fact that one individual is not some other individual. Thus Sancho, who was going to take the world by storm, dwindles to a clerk in a passport office.

At one point, he relates with much unction and great self-enjoyment that he does not become replete when the Japanese Emperor eats, because his stomach and that of the Japanese Emperor are "unique", "incomparable stomachs", i.e., not the *same* stomachs. If Sancho believes that in this way he has abolished the social relations hitherto existing or even only the laws of nature, then his *naïveté* is excessively great and it springs merely from the fact that philosophers have not depicted social relations as the mutual relations of particular individuals identical with themselves, and the laws of nature as the mutual connections of these particular bodies.

The classic expression which Leibniz gave to this old proposition (to be found on the first page of any physics textbook as the theory of the impenetrability of bodies) is well known:

"However, every monad necessarily differs from every other; for in nature there are never two things that exactly coincide with each other."[144]

Sancho's uniqueness is here reduced to a quality which he shares with every louse and every grain of sand.

The greatest disclaimer with which his philosophy could end is that it regards the realisation that Sancho is not Bruno, which is obvious to every country bumpkin and police sergeant, to be one of the greatest discoveries, and that it considers the fact of this difference to be a real miracle.

Thus the "critical hurrah" of our "virtuoso of thought" has become an uncritical *miserere*.[145]

---

144 In Leibniz's Monadology, a "monad" is an irreducibly simple substance — an elementary particle, a bit like an atom.

145 Latin for "have mercy" — often used to refer to Psalm 51, which was ostensibly written by David after he sinned with Bathsheba.

3. BOILING DOWN EVERYTHING AS FAR AS IT WILL GO: ABRIDGEMENT OF MY ABRIDGEMENT

1. Materialism as Philosophical Therapy

(1) Once upon a time a valiant fellow had the idea that men were drowned in water only because they were possessed with the *idea of gravity*. If they were to knock this notion out of their heads, say by stating it to be a superstition, a religious concept, they would be sublimely proof against any danger from water. His whole life long he fought against the illusion of gravity, of whose harmful results all statistics brought him new and manifold evidence. This valiant fellow was the type of the new revolutionary philosophers in Germany.

(2) The entire body of German philosophical criticism from Strauss to Stirner is confined to criticism of religious conceptions. The critics started from real religion and actual theology. What religious consciousness and a religious conception really meant was determined variously as they went along. Their advance consisted in subsuming the allegedly dominant metaphysical, political, juridical, moral and other conceptions under the class of religious or theological conceptions; and similarly in pronouncing political, juridical, moral consciousness as religious or theological, and the political, juridical, moral man — "*man*" in the last resort — as religious. The dominance of religion was taken for granted. Gradually every dominant relationship was pronounced a religious relationship and

transformed into a cult, a cult of law, a cult of the State, etc. On all sides it was only a question of dogmas and belief in dogmas. The world was sanctified to an ever-increasing extent till at last our venerable Saint Max was able to canonise it *en bloc* and thus dispose of it once for all.

This demand to change consciousness amounts to a demand to interpret reality in another way, i.e., to recognise it by means of another interpretation. The Young Hegelian ideologists, in spite of their allegedly "world-shattering" statements, are the staunchest conservatives. The most recent of them have found the correct expression for their activity when they declare they are only fighting against "*phrases*". They forget, however, that to these phrases they themselves are only opposing other phrases, and that they are in no way combating the real existing world when they are merely combating the phrases of this world.

It has not occurred to any one of these philosophers to inquire into the connection of German philosophy with German reality, the relation of their criticism to their own material surroundings.

(3) The premises from which we begin are not arbitrary ones, not dogmas, but real premises from which abstraction can only be made in the imagination. They are the real individuals, their activity and the material conditions of their life, both those which they find already existing and those produced by their activity. These premises can thus be verified in a purely empirical way.

The first premise of all human history is, of course, the existence of living human individuals. Thus the first fact to be established is the physical organisation of these individuals and their consequent relation to the rest of nature.

Men can be distinguished from animals by consciousness, by religion or anything else you like. They themselves begin to distinguish themselves from animals as soon as they begin to produce their means of subsistence, a step which is conditioned by their physical organisation. By producing their means of subsistence men are indirectly producing their material life.

The way in which men produce their means of subsistence depends first of all on the nature of the means of subsistence they actually find in existence and have to reproduce. This mode of production must not be considered simply as being the reproduction of the physical existence of the individuals. Rather it is a definite form of activity of these individuals, a definite form of expressing their life, a definite mode of life on their part. As individuals express their life, so they are. What they are, therefore, coincides with their production, both with what they produce and with *how* they produce. Hence what individuals are depends on the material conditions of their production.

This production only makes its appearance with the increase of population. In its turn this presupposes the *intercourse* of individuals with one another. The form of this intercourse is again determined by production.

The fact is, therefore, that definite individuals who are productively active in a definite way enter into these definite social and political relations. Empirical observation must in each separate instance bring out empirically, and without any mystification and speculation, the connection of the social and political structure with production. The social structure and the State are continually evolving out of the life-process of definite individuals, but of individuals, not as they may appear in their own or other people's imagination, but as they *really* are — i.e., as they operate, produce materially, and hence as they work under definite material limits, presuppositions and conditions independent of their will.

The production of ideas, of conceptions, of consciousness, is at first directly interwoven with the material activity and the material intercourse of men, the language of real life. Conceiving, thinking, the mental intercourse of men, appear at this stage as the direct efflux of their material behaviour. The same applies to mental production as expressed in the language of politics, laws, morality, religion, metaphysics, etc., of a people. Men are the producers of their conceptions, ideas, etc. — real, active men, as they are conditioned by a definite development of their productive forces and of the intercourse corresponding to these, up to its furthest forms. Consciousness can never be anything else than conscious existence, and the existence of men is their actual life-process. If in all ideology men and their circumstances appear upside-down as in a *camera obscura*, this phenomenon arises just as much from their historical life-process as the inversion of objects on the retina does from their physical life-process.

In direct contrast to German philosophy which descends from heaven to earth, here we ascend from earth to heaven. That is to say, we do not set out from what men say, imagine, conceive, nor from men as narrated, thought of, imagined, conceived, in order to arrive at men in the flesh. We set out from real, active men, and on the basis of their real life-process we demonstrate the development of the ideological reflexes and echoes of this life-process. The phantoms formed in the human brain are also, necessarily, sublimates of their material life-process, which is empirically verifiable and bound to material premises. Morality, religion, metaphysics, all the rest of ideology and their corresponding forms of consciousness, thus no longer retain the semblance of independence. They have no history, no development; but men, developing their material production and their material intercourse, alter, along with this their real existence, their thinking and the products of their thinking. Life is not determined by consciousness, but consciousness by life. In the first method of approach the starting-point is consciousness taken as the living individual; in the second method, which conforms to real life, it is the real living individuals themselves, and consciousness is considered solely as *their* consciousness.

This method of approach is not devoid of premises. It starts out from the real premises and does not abandon them for a moment. Its premises are men, not in any fantastic isolation and rigidity, but in their actual, empirically perceptible process of development under definite conditions. As soon as this active life-process is described, history ceases to be a collection of dead facts as it is with the empiricists (themselves still abstract), or an imagined activity of imagined subjects, as with the idealists.

Where speculation ends — in real life — there real, positive science begins: the representation of the practical activity, of the practical process of development of men. Empty talk about consciousness ceases, and real knowledge has to take its place.

(4) Communism is for us not a *state of affairs* which is to be established, an ideal to which reality will have to adjust itself. We call communism the *real* movement which abolishes the present state of things. The conditions of this movement result from the premises now in existence.

(5) The ideas of the ruling class are in every epoch the ruling ideas, i.e., the class which is the ruling *material* force of society, is at the same time its ruling *intellectual* force. The class which has the means of material production at its disposal, has control at the same time over the means of mental production, so that thereby, generally speaking,

the ideas of those who lack the means of mental production are subject to it. The ruling ideas are nothing more than the ideal expression of the dominant material relationships, the dominant material relationships grasped as ideas; hence of the relationships which make the one class the ruling one, therefore, the ideas of its dominance. The individuals composing the ruling class possess among other things consciousness, and therefore think. Insofar, therefore, as they rule as a class and determine the extent and compass of an epoch, it is self-evident that they do this in its whole range, hence among other things rule also as thinkers, as producers of ideas, and regulate the production and distribution of the ideas of their age: thus their ideas are the ruling ideas of the epoch. For instance, in an age and in a country where royal power, aristocracy, and bourgeoisie are contending for mastery and where, therefore, mastery is shared, the doctrine of this separation of powers proves to be the dominant idea and is expressed as an "eternal law".

If now in considering the course of history we detach the ideas of the ruling class from the ruling class itself and attribute to them an independent existence, if we confine ourselves to saying that these or those ideas were dominant at a given time, without bothering ourselves about the conditions of production and the producers of these ideas, if we thus ignore the individuals and world conditions which are the source of the ideas, we can say, for instance, that during the time that the aristocracy was dominant, the concepts honour, loyalty, etc., were dominant, during the dominance of the bourgeoisie the concepts freedom, equality, etc. The ruling class itself on the whole imagines this to be so. This conception of history, which is common to all historians, particularly since the eighteenth century, will necessarily come up against the phenomenon that increasingly abstract ideas hold sway, i.e., ideas which increasingly take on the form of universality. For each new class which puts itself in the place of one ruling before it, is compelled, merely in order to carry through its aim, to represent its interest as the common interest of all the members of society, that is, expressed in ideal form: it has to give its ideas the form of universality, and represent them as the only rational, universally valid ones. The class making a revolution appears from the very start, if only because it is opposed to a class, not as a class but as the representative of the whole of society; it appears as the whole mass of society confronting the one ruling class. It can do this because, to start with, its interest really is more connected with the common interest of all other non-ruling classes, because under the pressure of hitherto existing conditions its interest has not yet been able to develop as the particular interest of a particular class. Its victory, therefore, benefits also many individuals of the other classes which are not winning a dominant position, but only insofar as it now puts these individuals in a position to raise themselves into the ruling class. When the French bourgeoisie overthrew the power of the aristocracy, it thereby made it possible for many proletarians to raise themselves above the proletariat, but only insofar as they become bourgeois. Every new class, therefore, achieves its hegemony only on a broader basis than that of the class ruling previously, whereas the opposition of the non-ruling class against the new ruling class later develops all the more sharply and profoundly. Both these things determine the fact that the struggle to be waged against this new ruling class, in its turn, aims at a more decided and radical negation of the previous conditions of society than could all previous classes which sought to rule.

This whole semblance, that the rule of a certain class is only the rule of certain ideas, comes to a natural end, of course, as soon as class rule in general ceases to be the form in which society is organised, that is to say, as soon as it is no longer necessary to represent a particular interest as general or the "general interest" as ruling.

(6) Individuals have always built on themselves, but naturally on themselves within their given historical conditions and relationships, not on the "pure" individual in the sense of the ideologists. But in the course of historical evolution, and precisely through the inevitable fact that within the division of labour social relationships take on an independent existence, there appears a division within the life of each individual, insofar as it is personal and insofar as it is determined by some branch of labour and the conditions pertaining to it. The division between the personal and the class individual, the accidental nature of the conditions of life for the individual, appears only with the emergence of the class, which is itself a product of the bourgeoisie. This accidental character is only engendered and developed by competition and the struggle of individuals among themselves. Thus, in imagination, individuals seem freer under the dominance of the bourgeoisie than before, because their conditions of life seem accidental; in reality, of course, they are less free, because they are more subjected to the violence of things. The difference from the estate comes out particularly in the antagonism between the bourgeoisie and the proletariat. When the estate of the urban burghers, the corporations, etc., emerged in opposition to the landed nobility, their condition of existence — movable property and craft labour, which had already existed latently before their separation from the feudal ties — appeared as something positive, which was asserted against feudal landed property, and, therefore, in its own way at first took on a feudal form. Certainly the refugee serfs treated their previous servitude as something accidental to their personality. But here they only were doing what every class that is freeing itself from

a fetter does; and they did not free themselves as a class but separately. Moreover, they did not rise above the system of estates, but only formed a new estate, retaining their previous mode of labour even in their new situation, and developing it further by freeing it from its earlier fetters, which no longer corresponded to the development already attained.

For the proletarians, on the other hand: the condition of their existence — labour — and with it all the conditions of existence governing modern society, have become something accidental, something over which they, as separate individuals, have no control, and over which no social organisation can give them control. The contradiction between the individuality of each separate proletarian and labour, the condition of life forced upon him, becomes evident to him himself, for he is sacrificed from youth upwards and, within his own class, has no chance of arriving at the conditions which would place him in the other class.

Thus, while the refugee serfs only wished to be free to develop and assert those conditions of existence which were already there, and hence, in the end, only arrived at free labour, the proletarians, if they are to assert themselves as individuals, will have to abolish the very condition of their existence hitherto (which has, moreover, been that of all society up to the present), namely, labour. Thus they find themselves directly opposed to the form in which, hitherto, the individuals, of which society consists, have given themselves collective expression, that is, the State. In order, therefore, to assert themselves as individuals, they must overthrow the State.

Communism differs from all previous movements in that it overturns the basis of all earlier relations of production and intercourse, and for the first time consciously treats all natural premises as the creatures of hitherto existing men, strips them of their natural character and subjugates them to the power of the united individuals. Its organisation is, therefore, essentially economic, the material production of the conditions of this unity; it turns existing conditions into conditions of unity. The reality, which communism is creating, is precisely the true basis for rendering it impossible that anything should exist independently of individuals, insofar as reality is only a product of the preceding intercourse of individuals themselves.

Both for the production on a mass scale of this communist consciousness, and for the success of the cause itself, the alteration of men on a mass scale is, necessary, an alteration which can only take place in a practical movement, a revolution; this revolution is necessary, therefore, not only because the ruling class cannot be overthrown in any other way, but also because the class overthrowing it can only in a revolution succeed because in ridding itself of all the muck of ages and become fitted to found society anew.

2. Critique of Stirner's Critique of Political Liberalism

(1) The state of affairs in Germany at the end of the last century is fully reflected in Kant's *Critique of Practical Reason*. While the French bourgeoisie, by means of the most colossal revolution that history has ever known, was achieving domination and conquering the continent of Europe, while the already politically emancipated English bourgeoisie was revolutionising industry and subjugating India politically, and all the rest of the world commercially, the impotent German burghers did not get any further than "good will". Kant was satisfied with "good will" alone, even if it remained entirely without result, and he transferred the *realisation* of this good will, the harmony between it and the needs and impulses of individuals, to *the world beyond*.

(2) Kant's good will fully corresponds to the impotence, depression and wretchedness of the German burghers, whose petty interests were never capable of developing into the common, national interests of a class and who were, therefore, constantly exploited by the bourgeois of all other nations. These petty, local interests had as their counterpart, on the one hand, the truly local and provincial narrow-mindedness of the German burghers and, on the other hand, their cosmopolitan swollen-headedness. In general, from the time of the Reformation German development has borne a completely petty-bourgeois character. The old feudal aristocracy was, for the most part, annihilated in the peasant wars; what remained of it were either imperial petty princes who gradually achieved a certain independence and aped the absolute monarchy on a minute, provincial scale, or lesser landowners who partly squandered their little bit of property at the tiny courts, and then gained their livelihood from petty positions in the small armies and government offices — or, finally, Junkers from the backwoods, who lived a life of which even the most modest English *squire* or French *gentilhomme de province* would have been ashamed. Agriculture was carried on by a method which was neither parcellation nor large-scale production, and which, despite the preservation of feudal dependence and corvées, never drove the peasants to seek emancipation, both because this method of farming did not allow the emergence of any active revolutionary class and because of the absence of the revolutionary bourgeoisie corresponding to such a peasant class.

As regards the middle class, we can only emphasise here a few significant factors. It is significant that linen manufacture, i.e., an industry based on the spinning wheel and the hand-loom, came to be of some importance in Germany at the very time when in England those cumbersome tools were already being ousted by machines. Most characteristic of all is the position of the German middle class in relation to *Holland*. Holland, the only part of the Hanseatic League that became commercially important, tore itself free, cut Germany off from world trade except for two ports (Hamburg and Bremen) and since then dominated the whole of German trade. The German middle class was too impotent to set limits to exploitation by the Dutch. The bourgeoisie of little Holland, with its well-developed class interests, was more powerful than the far more numerous German middle class with its indifference and its divided petty interests. The fragmentation of interests was matched by the fragmentation of political organisation, the division into small principalities and free imperial cities. How could political concentration arise in a country which lacked all the economic conditions for it?

The impotence of each separate sphere of life (one can speak here neither of estates nor of classes, but at most of former estates and classes not yet born) did not allow any one of them to gain exclusive domination. The inevitable consequence was that during the epoch of absolute monarchy, which assumed here its most stunted, semi-patriarchal form, the special sphere which, owing to division of labour, was responsible for the administration of public interests acquired an abnormal independence, which became still greater in the bureaucracy of modern times. Thus, the state built itself up into an apparently independent force, and this position, which in other countries was only transitory — a transition stage — it has maintained in Germany until the present day. This position of the state explains both the conscientiousness of the civil servant, which is found nowhere else, and all the illusions about the state which are current in Germany, as well as the apparent independence of German theoreticians in relation to the middle class — the seeming contradiction between the form in which these theoreticians express the interests of the middle class and these interests themselves.

The characteristic form which French liberalism, based on real class interests, assumed in Germany we find again in Kant. Neither he, nor the German middle class, whose whitewashing spokesman he was, noticed that these theoretical ideas of the bourgeoisie had as their basis material interests and a *will* that was conditioned and determined by the material relations of production. Kant, therefore, separated this theoretical expression from the interests which it expressed; he made the materially motivated determinations of the will of the French bourgeois into pure self-determinations of "*free will*", of the will in and for itself, of the human will, and so converted it into purely ideological conceptual determinations and moral postulates. Hence the German petty bourgeois recoiled in horror from the practice of this energetic bourgeois liberalism as soon as this practice showed itself, both in the Reign of Terror and in shameless bourgeois profit-making.

Under the rule of Napoleon, the German middle class pushed its petty trade and its great illusions still further. As regards the petty-trading spirit which predominated in Germany at that time, Saint Sancho can, *inter alia*, compare Jean Paul, to mention only works of fiction, since they are the only source open to him. The German citizens, who railed against Napoleon for compelling them to drink chicory and for disturbing their peace with military billeting and recruiting of conscripts, reserved all their moral indignation for Napoleon and all their admiration for England; yet Napoleon rendered them the greatest services by cleaning out Germany's Augean stables and establishing civilised means of communication, whereas the English only waited for the opportunity to exploit them *à tort et à travers*. In the same petty-bourgeois spirit the German princes imagined they were fighting for the principle of legitimism and against revolution, whereas they were only the paid mercenaries of the English bourgeoisie. In the atmosphere of these universal illusions it was quite in the order of things that the estates privileged to cherish illusions — ideologists, school-masters, students, members of the *Tugendbund* — should talk big and give a suitable high-flown expression to the universal mood of fantasy and indifference. The political forms corresponding to a developed bourgeoisie were passed on to the Germans from outside by the July revolution — as we mention only a few main points we omit the intermediary period. Since German economic relations had by no means reached the stage of development to which these political forms corresponded, the middle class accepted them merely as abstract ideas, principles valid in and for themselves, pious wishes and phrases, Kantian self-determinations of the will and of human beings as they ought to be. Consequently their attitude to these forms was far more moral and disinterested than that of other nations, i.e., they exhibited a highly peculiar narrow-mindedness and remained unsuccessful in all their endeavours.

Finally the ever more powerful foreign competition and world intercourse — from which it became less and less possible for Germany to stand aside — compelled the diverse local interests in Germany to adopt some sort of common attitude. Particularly since 1840, the German middle class began to think about safeguarding these common interests; its attitude became national and liberal and it demanded protective tariffs and constitutions. Thus it has now got almost as far as the French bourgeoisie in 1789.

(3) If, like the Berlin ideologists, one judges liberalism and the state within the framework of local German impressions, or limits oneself merely to criticism of German-bourgeois illusions about liberalism, instead of seeing the correlation

of liberalism with the real interests from which it originated and without which it cannot really exist — then, of course, one arrives at the most banal conclusions. This German liberalism, in the form in which it expressed itself up to the most recent period, is, as we have seen, even in its popular form, empty enthusiasm, ideological reflections about *real* liberalism. How easy it is, therefore, to transform its content wholly into philosophy, into pure conceptual determinations, into "rational cognition"! Hence if one is so unfortunate as to know even this bourgeoisified liberalism only in the sublimated form given it by Hegel and the school-masters who depend on him, then one will arrive at conclusions belonging exclusively to the sphere of the holy. Sancho will provide us with a pitiful example of this.

Recently, in active circles, so much has been said about the rule of the bourgeois, that it is not surprising that news of it has even penetrated to Berlin, and there attracted the attention of easy-going school-masters. It cannot, however, be said that "Stirner" in his method of appropriating current ideas has adopted a particularly fruitful and profitable style — as was already evident from his exploitation of Hegel and will now be further exemplified.

It has not escaped our school-master that in recent times the liberals have been identified with the bourgeois. Since Saint Max identifies the bourgeois with the good burghers, with the petty German burghers, he does not grasp what has been transmitted to him as it is in fact and as it is expressed by all competent authors — viz., that the liberal phrases are the idealistic expression of the real interests of the bourgeoisie — but, on the contrary, as meaning that the final goal of the bourgeois is to become a perfect liberal, a citizen of the state. For Saint Max the bourgeois is not the truth of the *citoyen*, but the *citoyen* the truth of the bourgeois. This conception, which is as holy as it is German, goes to such lengths that "the middle class" (it should read:

"the domination of the bourgeoisie") is transformed into a "thought, nothing but a thought" and "the state" comes forward as the "true man", who in the "Rights of Man" confers the rights of "Man", the true solemnisation on each individual bourgeois. Hence he can transform the bourgeois — having separated the bourgeois as a liberal from the empirical bourgeois — into a holy liberal, just as he transforms the state into the "holy", and the relation of the bourgeois to the modern state into a holy relation, into a cult — and with this, in effect, he concludes his criticism of political liberalism. He has transformed it into the "holy".

3. Critique of Stirner's Critique of Communism

(1) The *modern* state, the rule of the bourgeoisie, is based on *freedom of labour*. The idea that along with freedom of religion, state, thought, etc., and hence "occasionally" "also" "perhaps" with freedom of *labour*, not I become free, but only one of my enslavers — this idea was borrowed by Saint Max himself, many times, though in a very distorted form, from the *Deutsch-Französische Jahrbücher*. Freedom of labour is free competition of the workers among themselves. Saint Max is very unfortunate in political economy as in all *other* spheres. Labour *is* free in all civilised countries; it is not a matter of freeing labour but of abolishing it.

(2) After "Stirner" has transferred property to "society", all the members of this society in his eyes at once become paupers and ragamuffins, although — even according to his idea of the communist order of things — they "own" the "supreme owner".

His benevolent proposal to the communists — "to transform the word 'ragamuffin' into an honourable form of address, just as the revolution did with the word 'citizen'" — is a striking example of how he confuses communism with something which long ago passed away. The revolution even "transformed" the word *sans culotte* "into an honourable form of address," as against "*honnêtes gens*", which he translates very inadequately as "good citizens".

Saint Sancho notes that the "elevation of society to supreme owner" is a "second *robbery* of the personal element in the interests of humanity," while communism is only the completed robbery of the "robbery of the personal element." "Since he unquestionably regards robbery as detestable," Saint Sancho "therefore believes for example," that he "has branded" communism "already by the" above "proposition". Once 'Stirner' has detected "even robbery" in communism, how could he fail to feel "profound disgust" at it and "just indignation"? We now challenge "Stirner" to name a bourgeois who has written about communism (or Chartism) and has not put forward the same absurdity with great emphasis. Communism will certainly carry out "robbery" of what the bourgeois regards as "personal".

(3) Saint Max calmly utters the great historic words:

> "Human beings, by no means intending to achieve their own development, have always wanted to form a society."

Human beings, by no means wanting to form a society, have, nevertheless, only achieved the development of society, because they have always wanted to develop only as isolated individuals and therefore achieved their own development only in and through society. Incidentally it would only occur to a saint of the type of our Sancho to separate the development of "human beings" from the development of the "society" in which they live, and then let his fantasy roam on this fantastic basis. Incidentally, he has forgotten his own proposition, inspired by Saint

Bruno, in which just previously he set people the moral demand of changing themselves and thereby changing their society — a proposition, therefore, in which he identifies the development of people with the development of their society.

(4) With "Stirner", "communism" begins with searchings for "essence"; being a good "youth" he wants again only to "penetrate behind things." That communism is a highly practical movement, pursuing practical aims by practical means, and that only perhaps in Germany, in opposing the German philosophers, can it spare a moment for the problem of "essence" — this, of course, is of no concern to our saint. This Stirnerian "communism", which yearns so much for "essence", arrives, therefore, only at a philosophical category, i.e., "being-for-one-another", which then by means of a few arbitrary equations...

Being-for-one-another = to exist *only* through another
= to exist as a worker
= universal community of workers

... is brought somewhat closer to the empirical world.

As universal community of workers, Saint Max reduces the whole of communism to equal wages. "Against competition," Stirner states, "there rises the principle of the society of ragamuffins — *distribution*. Is it possible then," Stirner asks, "that I, who am very resourceful, should have no advantage over one who is resourceless?" Further, he speaks of a "universal tax on human activity in communist society." Finally, he ascribes to the communists the view that "labour" is "the only resource" of man. Thus, Saint Max re-introduces into communism private property in its dual form — as distribution and wage-labour. As before in connection with "robbery", Saint Max here again displays the most ordinary and narrow-minded bourgeois views as "his own" "penetrations" into the essence of communism. As a real petty bourgeois, he is then afraid that he, "who is very resourceful... should have no advantage over one who is resourceless" — although he *should* fear nothing so much as being left to his own "resources".

Incidentally, he "who is very resourceful" imagines that citizenship is a matter of indifference to the proletarians, after he has first assumed that they *have* it. This is just as he imagined above that for the bourgeoisie the form of government is a matter of indifference. The workers attach so much importance to citizenship, i.e., to *active* citizenship, that where they have it, for instance in America, they "make good use" of it, and where they do not *have* it, they strive to obtain it. Compare the proceedings of the North American workers at innumerable meetings, the whole history of English Chartism, and of French communism and reformism.

(5) How deeply our saint has "penetrated" into the essence of communism is evident also from the fact that he ascribes to communism the desire to bring about "true well-being" in the shape of "honestly earned enjoyment". Who, except "Stirner" and a few Berlin cobblers and tailors, thinks of "honestly earned enjoyment"?! Who, except "Stirner", is able to attribute such moral absurdities to the immoral revolutionary proletarians, who, as the whole civilised world knows (Berlin, of course, does not belong to the civilised world), have the wicked intention not "honestly to earn" their "enjoyment" but to take it by conquest! And, what is more, to put this into the mouth of communists, for whom the basis of this whole opposition between work and enjoyment disappears. Let our highly moral saint put his mind at rest on this score. "Honest earning" will be left to him and those whom, unknown to himself, he

represents — his petty handicrafts-men who have been ruined by industrial freedom and are morally "indignant". "Enjoyable idleness", too, belongs wholly to the most trivial bourgeois outlook. But the crowning point of the whole statement is the artful bourgeois scruple that he raises against the communists: that they want to abolish the "well-being" of the rentier and yet talk about the "well-being of all". Consequently, he believes that in communist society there will still be rentiers, whose 'well-being' would have to be abolished. He asserts that 'well-being' *as rentier* is inherent in the individuals who are at present rentiers, that it is inseparable from their individuality, and he imagines that for these individuals there can exist no other 'well-being' than that which is determined by their position as rentiers.

He believes further that a society which has still to wage a struggle against rentiers and the like, is already organised in a communist way. And finally he makes the moral demand that the communists should quietly allow themselves to be exploited to all eternity by rentiers, merchants, factory-owners, etc., because they cannot abolish this exploitation without at the same time destroying the "well-being" of these gentlemen. *Jacques le bonhomme*, who poses here as the champion of the gros-bourgeois, can save himself the trouble of preaching moralising sermons to the communists, who can every day hear much better ones from his "good burghers". The communists, at any rate, will have no scruples about overthrowing the rule of the bourgeoisie and abolishing its "well-being", as soon as they are strong enough to do so. It does not matter to them at all whether this "well-being" common to their enemies and determined by class relations also appeals as personal "well-being" to a sentimentality which is narrow-mindedly presumed to exist. The "well-being" which the rentier enjoys as rentier is not the "well-being" of the individual as such, but of the rentier, not an individual well-being but a well-being that is general within the framework of the class.

When the narrow-minded bourgeois says to the communists: by abolishing property, i.e., my existence as a capitalist, as a landed proprietor, as a factory-owner, and your existence as workers, you abolish my individuality and your own; by making it impossible for me to exploit you, the workers, to rake in my profit, interest or rent, you make it impossible for me to exist as an individual. — When, therefore, the bourgeois tells the communists: by abolishing my existence as a *bourgeois*, you abolish my existence as an *individual*; when thus he identifies himself as a bourgeois with himself as an individual, one must, at least, recognise his frankness and shamelessness. For the bourgeois it is actually the case, he believes himself to be an individual only insofar as he is a bourgeois.

But when the theoreticians of the bourgeoisie come forward and give a general expression to this assertion, when they equate the bourgeois's property with individuality in theory as well and want to give a logical justification for this equation, then this nonsense begins to become solemn and holy.

Stirner's arguments regarding the impossibility of abolishing private property depend on his transforming private property into the concept of property, on exploiting the etymological connection between the words *property* [*Eigentum*] and *own* [*eigen*] and declaring the word *own* an eternal truth, because even under the communist system it could happen that a stomach-ache will be *own* to him. All this theoretical nonsense, which seeks refuge in etymology, would be impossible if the actual private property that the communists want to abolish had not been transformed into the abstract notion of "property". This transformation, on the one hand, saves one the trouble of having to say anything, or even merely to know anything, about actual private property and, on the other hand, makes it easy to discover a contradiction in communism, since *after* the abolition of (*actual*) property it is, of course, easy to discover all sorts of things in communism which can be included in the concept "property".

In reality, of course, the situation is just the reverse. Actual private property is something extremely general which has nothing at all to do with individuality, which indeed directly nullifies individuality. Insofar as I am regarded as a property-owner I am not regarded as an individual — a statement which is corroborated every day by the marriages for money. In reality I possess private property only insofar as I have something vendible, whereas what is *peculiar* to me may not be vendible at all. My frock-coat is private property for me only so long as I can barter, pawn or sell it, so long as it is marketable. If it loses that feature, if it becomes tattered, it can still have a number of features which make it valuable *for me*, it may even become a feature of me and turn me into a tatterdemalion. But no economist would think of classing it as my private property, since it does not enable me to command any, even the smallest, amount of other people's labour. A lawyer, an ideologist of private property, could perhaps still indulge in such twaddle. Private property *alienates* the individuality not only of people but also of things. Land has nothing to do with rent of land, the machine has nothing to do with profit. For the landed proprietor, land has the significance only of rent of land; he leases his plots of land and receives rent; this is a feature which land can lose without losing a single one of its inherent features, without, for example, losing any part of its fertility; it is a feature the extent and even the existence of which depends on social relations which are created and destroyed without the assistance of individual landed proprietors. It is the same with machines.

In a word, rent of land, profit, etc., these actual forms of existence of private property, are *social relations* corresponding to a definite stage of production, and they are *"individual"* only so long as they have not become fetters on the existing productive forces.

(6) *Communism* is quite incomprehensible to our saint because the communists do not oppose egoism to selflessness or selflessness to egoism, nor do they express this contradiction theoretically either in its sentimental or in its high-flown ideological form; they rather demonstrate its material source, with which it disappears of itself. The communists do not preach morality at all, as Stirner does so extensively. They do not put to people the moral demand: love one another, do not be egoists, etc.; on the contrary, they are very well aware that egoism, just as much as selflessness, is in definite circumstances a necessary form of the self-assertion of individuals.

Hence, the communists by no means want, as Saint Max believes, to do away with the "private individual" for the sake of the "general", selfless man. That is a figment of the imagination concerning which one could already have found the necessary explanation in the *Deutsch-Französische Jahrbücher*. Communist theoreticians, the only communists who have time to devote to the study of history, are distinguished precisely by the fact that they alone have discovered that throughout history the "general interest" is created by individuals who are defined as "private persons". They know that this contradiction is only a seeming one because one side of it, what is called the "general interest", is constantly being produced by the other side, private interest, and in relation to the latter it is by no means an independent force with an independent history — so that this contradiction is in practice constantly destroyed and reproduced. Hence it is not a question of the Hegelian "negative unity" of two sides of a contradiction, but of the materially determined destruction of the preceding materially determined mode of life of individuals, with the disappearance of which this contradiction together with its unity also disappears.

4. From Egoism to Communism

(1) Stirner regards the various stages of life only as "self-discoveries"; of the individual, and these "self-discoveries" are moreover always reduced to a definite relation of *consciousness*. Thus the variety of consciousness is here the life of the individual. The physical and social changes which take place in the individuals and produce an altered consciousness are, of course, of no concern to Stirner. In Stirner's work, therefore, child, youth and man always find the world ready-made, just as they merely "find" "themselves"; absolutely nothing is done to ensure that there should be something which can in fact be found. But even the relation of *consciousness* is not correctly understood either, but only in its speculative distortion. Hence, too, all these figures have a philosophical attitude to the world — "the child is *realistic*," "the youth is *idealistic*," the man is the negative unity of the two, absolute negativity, as is evident from the above-quoted final proposition. Here the secret of "a man's life" is revealed, here it becomes clear that the "*child*" was only a disguise of "*realism*", the "*youth*" a disguise of "*idealism*", the "*man*" of an attempted solution of this *philosophical antithesis*. This solution, this "*absolute negativity*", is arrived at — it is now seen — only thanks to the man blindly taking on trust the illusions both of the child and of the youth, *believing* thus to have overcome the world of things and the world of the spirit.

Since Saint Max pays no attention to the physical and social "life" of the individual, and says nothing at all about "life", he quite consistently abstracts from historical epochs, nationalities, classes, etc., or, which is the *same thing*, he inflates the *consciousness* predominant in the class nearest to him in his immediate environment into the normal consciousness of "a man's life". In order to rise above this local and pedantic narrow-mindedness he has only to confront "his" youth with the first young clerk he encounters, a young English factory worker or young Yankee, not to mention the young Kirghiz-Kazakhs.

Our saint's enormous gullibility — the true spirit of his book — is not content with causing his youth to believe in his child, and his man to believe in his youth. The illusions which some "youths", "men", etc., have or claim to have about themselves, are without any examination accepted by Stirner himself and confused with the "*life*", with the *reality*, of these highly ambiguous youths and men.

The prototype of the entire structure of the stages of life has already been depicted in the third part of Hegel's *Encyclopedia* and "in various transformations" in other passages in Hegel as well. Saint Max, pursuing "his own" purposes, had, of course, to undertake certain "transformations" here also. Whereas Hegel, for example, is still to such an extent guided by the empirical world that he portrays the German burgher as the servant of the world around him, Stirner has to make him the master of this world, which he is not even in imagination. Similarly, Saint Max pretends that he does not speak of the old man for empirical reasons; he wishes to wait until he becomes one himself (here, therefore, "a man's life" = his unique life). Hegel briskly sets about constructing the four stages of the human life because, in the real world, the negation is posited twice, i.e., as moon and as comet (cf. Hegel's *Philosophy of Nature*), and therefore the quaternity here takes the place of the trinity. Stirner finds his own uniqueness in making moon and comet coincide and so abolishes the unfortunate old man from "a man's life". The reason for this conjuring trick becomes evident as soon as we examine the construction of the unique history of man.

(2) Thus we see how the "egoist in agreement with himself" as opposed to the "egoist in the ordinary sense" and the "selfless egoist", is based from the outset on an illusion about both of these and about the real relations of real people. The representative of personal interests is merely an "egoist in the ordinary sense" because of his necessary contradiction to communal interests which, within the existing mode of production and intercourse, are given an independent existence as general interests and are conceived and vindicated in the form of ideal interests. The representative of the interests of the community is merely "selfless" because of his opposition to personal interests, fixed as private interests, and because the interests of the community are defined as general and ideal interests. Both the "selfless egoist" and the "egoist in the ordinary sense" coincide, in the final analysis, in self-denial.

Egoism in agreement with itself really endeavours to transform every man into a "secret police state". The spy and sleuth "reflection" keeps a strict eye on every impulse of spirit and body, and every deed and thought, every manifestation of life is, for him, a matter of reflection, i.e., a police matter. It is this dismemberment of man into "natural instinct" and "reflection" (the inner plebeian — creation; and the internal police — creator) which constitutes the egoist in agreement with himself.

(3) It depends not on *consciousness*, but on *being*; not on thought, but on life; it depends on the individual's empirical development and manifestation of life, which in turn depends on the conditions obtaining in the world. If the circumstances in which the individual lives allow him only

the one-sided development of one quality at the expense of all the rest, if they give him the material and time to develop only that one quality, then this individual achieves only a one-sided, crippled development. No moral preaching avails here. And the manner in which this one, pre-eminently favoured quality develops depends again, on the one hand, on the material available for its development and, on the other hand, on the degree and manner in which the other qualities are suppressed. Precisely because thought, for example, is the thought of a particular, definite individual, it remains his definite thought, determined by his individuality and the conditions in which he lives. The thinking individual therefore has no need to resort to prolonged reflection about thought as such in order to declare that his thought is his own thought, his property; from the outset it is his own, peculiarly determined thought and it was precisely his peculiarity which in the case of Saint Sancho was found to be the "opposite" of this, a peculiarity which is peculiarity "*as such*". In the case of an individual, for example, whose life embraces a wide circle of varied activities and practical relations to the world, and who, therefore, lives a many-sided life, thought has the same character of universality as every other manifestation of his life. Consequently, it neither becomes fixed in the form of abstract thought nor does it need complicated tricks of reflection when the individual passes from thought to some other manifestation of life. From the outset it is always a factor in the total life of the individual, one which disappears and is reproduced as required.

The only thing our saint achieves with the aid of his arduous reflection about his qualities and passions is that by his constant crotchetiness and scuffling with them he poisons the enjoyment and satisfaction of them.

(4) If the ego is divorced from all its empirical conditions of life, its activity, the conditions of its existence, if it is

separated from the world that forms its basis and from its own body, then, of course, it has no other vocation and no other designation than that of representing the Caius of the logical proposition and to assist Saint Sancho in arriving at the equations given above. In the real world, on the other hand, where individuals have needs, they thereby already have a vocation and task; and at the outset it is still immaterial whether they make this their vocation in their imagination as well. It is clear, however, that because the individuals possess consciousness they form an idea of this vocation which their empirical existence has given them and, thus, furnish Saint Sancho with the opportunity of seizing on the word vocation, that is, on the mental expression of their actual conditions of life, and of leaving out of account these conditions of life themselves.

The proletarian, for example, who like every human being has the vocation of satisfying his needs and who is not in a position to satisfy even the needs that he has in common with all human beings, the proletarian whom the necessity to work a 14-hour day debases to the level of a beast of burden, whom competition degrades to a mere thing, an article of trade, who from his position as a mere productive force, the sole position left to him, is squeezed out by other, more powerful productive forces — this proletarian is, if only for these reasons, confronted with the real task of revolutionising his conditions. He can, of course, imagine this to be his "vocation", he can also, if he likes to engage in propaganda, express his "vocation" by saying that to do this or that is the human vocation of the proletarian, the more so since his position does not even allow him to satisfy the needs arising directly from his human nature. Saint Sancho does not concern himself with the reality underlying this idea, with the practical aim of this proletarian — he clings to the word "vocation" and declares it to be the holy, and the proletarian to be a servant of the holy — the easiest way of considering himself superior and "proceeding further".

Particularly in the relations that have existed hitherto, when one class always ruled, when the conditions of life of an individual always coincided with the conditions of life of a class, when, therefore, the practical task of each newly emerging class was bound to appear to each of its members as a universal task, and when each class could actually overthrow its predecessor only by liberating the individuals of all classes from certain chains which had hitherto fettered them — under these circumstances it was essential that the task of the individual members of a class striving for domination should be described as a universal human task.

Incidentally, when for example the bourgeois tells the proletarian that his, the proletarian's, human task is to work fourteen hours a day, the proletarian is quite justified in replying in the same language that on the contrary his task is to overthrow the entire bourgeois system.

(5) When Saint Sancho is starving to death it is not due to lack of food, but to his own hungriness, his own quality of starving. If he falls out of a window and breaks his neck, it happens not because the force of gravity plunges him downwards, but because absence of wings, inability to fly, is a quality of his own.

In view of its extreme triviality and indisputable certainty, there should have been no need to mention the perfectly inoffensive proposition that the *idea* of man is not the *real* man, that the idea of a thing is not the thing itself — a proposition which is also applicable to a stone and to the idea of a stone, in accordance with which Sancho should have said that the real stone is non-stone. But Sancho's well-known fantasy that only because of the domination of ideas and concepts mankind has up to now been subjected to all sorts of misfortunes, makes it possible for him to link his old conclusions again with this proposition. Sancho's old opinion that one has only to get a few ideas out of one's head in order to abolish from the world the conditions which have given rise to these ideas, is reproduced here in the form that one has only to get out of one's *head* the idea of man in order to put an end to the actually existing conditions which are today called inhuman — whether this predicate "inhuman" expresses the opinion of the individual in contradiction with his conditions or the opinion of the normal, ruling society about the abnormal, subjected class. In just the same way, a whale taken from the ocean and put in the *Kupfergraben*, if it possessed consciousness, would declare this situation created by "unfavourable circumstances" to be unwhale-like, although Sancho could prove that it is whale-like, if only because it is its, the whale's, own situation — that is precisely how people argue in certain circumstances.

Sancho arrives at his uniqueness by getting "Man" out of his head. He thereby ceases "to think of himself only in comparison with someone else" and "to recognise something above him." He becomes incomparable. This is again the same old fantasy of Sancho's that it is not the needs of individuals, but concepts, ideas, "the holy" — here in the shape of "Man" — that are the sole *tertium comparationis* and the sole bond between individuals. Sancho, who notices nothing but "the holy", need not bother about the fact that it is through their needs that individuals are linked together, and that the development of the productive forces up to now implies the domination of one section over the other. He gets an idea out of his head and thereby becomes unique.

(6) The uniqueness, the originality, the "peculiar" development of individuals which, according to Sancho,

does not for example occur in all "human works", although no one will deny that one stove-setter does not set a stove in the "*same*" way as another; the "unique" development of individuals which, in the opinion of this same Sancho, does not occur in religious, political, etc., spheres, although no one will deny that of all those who believe in Islam not one believes in it in the "same" way as another and to this extent each of them is "unique", just as among citizens not one has the same attitude to the state as another if only because it is a matter of his attitude, and not that of some *other* — all this much praised "uniqueness" which (according to Sancho) was so distinct from "*sameness*", *identity of the person*, that in all individuals who have so far existed he could hardly see anything but "specimens" of a species, is thus reduced here to the identity of a person with himself, as established by the police, to the fact that one individual is not some other individual. Thus Sancho, who was going to take the world by storm, dwindles to a clerk in a passport office.

At one point, he relates with much unction and great self-enjoyment that he does not become replete when the Japanese Emperor eats, because his stomach and that of the Japanese Emperor are "unique", "incomparable stomachs", i.e., not the *same* stomachs. If Sancho believes that in this way he has abolished the social relations hitherto existing or even only the laws of nature, then his *naïveté* is excessively great and it springs merely from the fact that philosophers have not depicted social relations as the mutual relations of particular individuals identical with themselves, and the laws of nature as the mutual connections of these particular bodies.

The classic expression which Leibniz gave to this old proposition (to be found on the first page of any physics textbook as the theory of the impenetrability of bodies) is well known:

"However, every monad necessarily differs from every other; for in nature there are never two things that exactly coincide with each other."

Sancho's uniqueness is here reduced to a quality which he shares with every louse and every grain of sand.

The greatest disclaimer with which his philosophy could end is that it regards the realisation that Sancho is not Bruno, which is obvious to every country bumpkin and police sergeant, to be one of the greatest discoveries, and that it considers the fact of this difference to be a real miracle.

(7) Even that which constitutes the advantage of an individual as such over other individuals, is in our day at the same time a product of society and in its realisation is bound to assert itself as privilege, as we have already shown Sancho in connection with competition. Further, the individual as such, regarded by himself, is subordinated to division of labour, which makes him one-sided, cripples and determines him.

What, at best, does Sancho's sharpening of contradiction and abolition of the special amount to? To this, that the mutual relations of individuals should be their behaviour to one another, while their mutual differences should be their *self-distinctions* (as one empirical self distinguishes *itself* from another). Both of these are either, as with Sancho, an ideological paraphrase of *what exists*, for the relations of individuals under all circumstances can only be their mutual behaviour, while their differences can only be their self-distinctions. Or they are the pious wish that they *should* behave in *such a way* and differ from one another *in such a way*, that their behaviour does not acquire independent existence as a social relationship independent of them, and that their differences from one another should not assume the material character (independent of the person) which they have assumed and daily continue to assume.

Individuals have always and in all circumstances "proceeded *from themselves*", but since they were not *unique* in the sense of not needing any connections with one another, and since their needs, consequently their nature, and the method of satisfying their needs, connected them with one another (relations between the sexes, exchange, division of labour), they *had to* enter into relations with one another. Moreover, since they entered into intercourse with one another not as pure egos, but as individuals at a definite stage of development of their productive forces and requirements, and since this intercourse, in its turn, determined production and needs, it was, therefore, precisely the personal, individual behaviour of individuals, their behaviour to one another as individuals, that created the existing relations and daily reproduces them anew. They entered into intercourse with one another as what they were, they proceeded "from themselves", as they were, irrespective of their "outlook on life". This "outlook on life" — even the warped one of the philosophers — could, of course, only be determined by their actual life. Hence it certainly follows that the development of an individual is determined by the development of all the others with whom he is directly or indirectly associated, and that the different generations of individuals entering into relation with one another are connected with one another, that the physical existence of the later generations is determined by that of their predecessors, and that these later generations inherit the productive forces and forms of intercourse accumulated by their predecessors, their own mutual relations being determined thereby. In short, it is clear that development takes place and that the history of a single individual cannot possibly be separated from the history of preceding or contemporary individuals, but is determined by this history.

The transformation of the individual relationship into its opposite, a purely material relationship, the distinction of individuality and fortuity by the individuals themselves, is a historical process, as we have already shown, and at different stages of development it assumes different, ever sharper and more universal forms. In the present epoch, the domination of material relations over individuals, and the suppression of individuality by fortuitous circumstances, has assumed its sharpest and most universal form, thereby setting existing individuals a very definite task. It has set them the task of replacing the domination of circumstances and of chance over individuals by the domination of individuals over chance and circumstances. It has not, as Sancho imagines, put forward the demand that "I should develop myself", which up to now every individual has done without Sancho's good advice; it has on the contrary called for liberation from a quite definite mode of development. This task, dictated by present-day relations, coincides with the task of organising society in a communist way.

We have already shown above that the abolition of a state of affairs in which relations become independent of individuals, in which individuality is subservient to chance and the personal relations of individuals are subordinated to general class relations, etc. — that the abolition of this state of affairs is determined in the final analysis by the abolition of division of labour. We have also shown that the abolition of division of labour is determined by the development of intercourse and productive forces to such a degree of universality that private property and division of labour become fetters on them. We have further shown that private property can be abolished only on condition of an all-round development of individuals, precisely because the existing form of intercourse and the existing productive forces are all-embracing and only individuals that are developing in an all-round fashion can appropriate them, i.e., can turn them into free manifestations of their lives. We have shown that at the present time individuals *must* abolish private property, because the productive forces and forms of intercourse have developed so far that, under the domination of private property, they have become destructive forces, and because the contradiction between the classes has reached its extreme limit. Finally, we have shown that the abolition of private property and of the division of labour is itself the association of individuals on the basis created by modern productive forces and world intercourse.

Within communist society, the only society in which the genuine and free development of individuals ceases to be a mere phrase, this development is determined precisely by the connection of individuals, a connection which consists partly in the economic prerequisites and partly in the necessary solidarity of the free development of all, and, finally, in the universal character of the activity of individuals on the basis of the existing productive forces. We are, therefore, here concerned with individuals at a definite historical stage of development and by no means merely with individuals chosen at random, even disregarding the indispensable communist revolution, which itself is a general condition for their free development. The individuals' consciousness of their mutual relations will, of course, likewise be completely changed, and, therefore, will no more be the "principle of love" or *dévoûment* than it will be egoism.

Thus, "uniqueness" — taken in the sense of genuine development and individual behaviour, as outlined above — presupposes not only things quite different from good will and right consciousness, but even the direct opposite of Sancho's fantasies. With him "uniqueness" is nothing more than an embellishment of existing conditions, a little drop of comforting balm for the poor, impotent soul that has become wretched through wretchedness.

4. ABRIDGEMENT OF THE ABRIDGEMENT OF THE ABRIDGEMENT (FROM "THESES ON FEUERBACH")

The philosophers have only *interpreted* the world, in various ways; the point is to change it.

ACKNOWLEDGEMENTS

I first encountered *The German Ideology* as a graduate student at the University of Essex, teaching sections on it as the assistant on the "Capitalism and Its Critics" module, then led by Timo Jütten. It's possible that I had already read the "Feuerbach" chapter, in C.J. Arthur's abridgement, around the time I started my PhD the previous year — but at any rate, *teaching* the thing was when I first remember really *absorbing* it: actually realising what was going on. The early Marx was one of the three great revelations I experienced that second year studying for my PhD: the other two being Aristotle, as inculcated me — in quite openly Marxist mode — by David McNeill, who was supervising me that year; and Edie Miller, the love of my life, and now the mother of my children, Iggy and Ettie. This was the year I first started thinking deeply about what a "human being" is — which is probably also because it coincided with my first starting to feel like one.

What struck me most about communism, as presented in *The German Ideology*, was how *dynamic* it was supposed to be. I was raised at the so-called "End of History", in the wake of the collapse of Soviet Union. When I was growing up, "communism" was the name of a rigid, outmoded ideology, desperately wanting by the "verdict of history". A call for justice, perhaps, but an ill-articulated one, that had anyway been catastrophically misheard — a desire for something better, but which had only ended up leading to something worse. (And besides which, my dad used to tell me, all those Blairite ministers started off as student Stalinists, and now they're off invading Iraq — really they just want to *control* people, that's the problem. The left always think they know best, and blah blah blah.)

But clearly, in the Marx text I was now reading, "communism" meant something other than that. "Communism" was the name of a transformative relation between thought and world: "the real movement", as I read there, "that abolishes the present state of things" — perhaps, whatever "the present state of things" might, at any point *ever*, be. This was something more than just a "political ideology" — a theory of how the state ought to be organised — it was a new way of thinking, a new way of being. Perhaps this is another major reason *why* reading Marx coincided with my starting to feel like a person: he showed me how a human being *ought* to be engaged with their world. If "political philosophy", as typically taught in the academy in restricted, Rawlsian mode, was really just philosophy *posing* as politics, philosophy demurring donnishly from the point at which politics ought to be allowed to happen, like how all the academics at the bar after talks used to dither forever over choosing a table to sit at, then here we had politics as philosophy: an irreducibly political doctrine, reaching down to the realm of epistemology and metaphysics — giving vastly more convincing answers, than anything ostensibly politically "neutral".

The text too, fittingly, struck me as something dynamic. *The German Ideology* was unfinished — of course it was, even the most casual acquaintance with the chapter "on Feuerbach" reveals that Marx and Engels barely got around to mentioning the guy at all. But when you read the thing properly, and engage with it critically, you realise that this is hardly a *problem*. Precisely *insofar as* it is something rather loose and unfinished, the text becomes quite welcomingly approachable: far from quivering before it, as some eternal repository of quasi-Biblical socialist dogma, one becomes free to add one's own egg. In never having been finished by Marx and Engels, in never having been properly prepared for publication, *The German Ideology* has been left to *us* — to do with whatever we might need to. Riazanov was just the first of many editors: any engagement can be a revision.

Perhaps this sort of dynamism is why I first understood the text as I was teaching it — indeed, I have always found that *The German Ideology* is at its most powerful when being read in a seminar room. The seeds of the present edition were sown during the 2017-18 academic year, which I spent as a Teaching Fellow at the University of Warwick, during which I was — among other things — responsible for teaching a module on Marx and Hegel, to a very bright and engaged core of undergraduates. Among other things, it was during this period that I was first prompted — I think in response to a question from a student — to read and engage with the chapter on Stirner, which I had previously claimed the usual licence to ignore. Presumably I was also affected by the attitude of my closest superior at Warwick, Stephen Houlgate, whose very sincere enthusiasm for diligent scholarly work has a tendency to rub off on one.

Originally this was only supposed to be an article, which I wrote the first draft of very soon after I left Warwick and moved, unemployed, to Newcastle, on why exactly Marx and Engels had written such a lengthy critique of Stirner — as well as on the importance of Stirner's Egoism for understanding what Marx and Engels think "communism" is, and how it might ever be brought about. Hopefully by the time this edition comes out, that article will have seen the light of day. But at any rate: it was over the course of writing it that I realised that someone, at some point, really ought to produce a version of the Stirner chapter that might actually be *legible*. And it was also around this time that I became aware of a gathering scholarly consensus that *The*

German Ideology as we know it — for me, perhaps *the* single most valuable philosophical text in the canon — didn't really exist; that it had always been a phantom, a "spook", cleverly conjured up by a rogue group of Soviet editors. So I also became aware of a pressing need to find a way of challenging that reading — to stake a claim, somehow, for the validity of the text *as we know it*.

I always figured that my new, Stirner-incorporating, Feuerbach-chapter-salvaging abridgement of *The German Ideology* would be something I'd get round to producing *eventually*, maybe when (if) someone ever gave me a proper, full-time academic position. Unfortunately that hasn't happened yet — but perhaps the present edition has benefited from that, as I also haven't had to really stick to any *merely* academic strictures. Ultimately, I did it now because I figured I had time to, and I'd already published my first book, *Infinitely Full of Hope*, with Repeater, so it wasn't hard to persuade them to give me a contract (thanks as ever to Tariq Goddard and Josh Turner). During this period, I was also teaching part-time at the University of Hull — where unfortunately, I did not have any cause to teach Marx. Thanks are due, at any rate, to my colleagues there: especially Stephen Burwood and Dawn Wilson. I hope one day Philosophy at Hull can flourish anew.

A particular thanks is also due to Fabian Freyenhagen (who was also my primary PhD supervisor back in the day), Amelia Horgan and Dan Swain for their comments on the manuscript — which were both helpful, and reassuring. Charlotte Alderwick helped clarify a point about Schelling. Matteo Mandarini's much more critical comments were initially a lot more difficult to deal with — but hopefully the text is much stronger for my having grappled with them. Finally, credit to Matt Colquhoun for his careful, conscientious job of proofreading my originally much sloppier text.

REPEATER BOOKS

is dedicated to the creation of a new reality. The landscape of twenty-first-century arts and letters is faded and inert, riven by fashionable cynicism, egotistical self-reference and a nostalgia for the recent past. Repeater intends to add its voice to those movements that wish to enter history and assert control over its currents, gathering together scattered and isolated voices with those who have already called for an escape from Capitalist Realism. Our desire is to publish in every sphere and genre, combining vigorous dissent and a pragmatic willingness to succeed where messianic abstraction and quiescent co-option have stalled: abstention is not an option: we are alive and we don't agree.